DK EYEWITNESS TOP 10 TRAVEL GUIDES

HONG KONG

LIAM FITZPATRICK,
JASON GAGLIARDI AND
ANDREW STONE

DORLING KINDERSLEY
LONDON • NEW YORK • MUNICH
MELBOURNE • DELHI
WWW.DK.COM

Left **Star Ferry** Centre **Bird Market** Right **View from the Peak**

DK

LONDON, NEW YORK,
MELBOURNE, MUNICH AND DELHI
www.dk.com

Produced by
Blue Island Publishing, London

Reproduced by Colourscan, Singapore
Printed and bound in Italy by Graphicom

First published in Great Britain in 2002
by Dorling Kindersley Limited
80 Strand, London WC2R 0RL
A Penguin Company

**Copyright 2002, 2004 © Dorling
Kindersley Limited, London**

A CIP catalogue record is available from
the British Library.

UK ISBN 0 4053 0804 4

Within each Top 10 list in this book, no
hierarchy of quality or popularity is
implied. All 10 are, in the editor's
opinion, of roughly equal merit.

Contents

Hong Kong's Top 10

Left **Ten Thousand Buddhas Temple** Centre **Lantau** Right **Window of the World, Shenzhen**

Left **Hong Kong skyline** Right **Temple guardian deity**

Following pages **Central district at night**

HONG KONG'S TOP 10

🔟 Hong Kong's Highlights

"A dream of Manhattan, arising from the South China Sea." For succinctness, modern travel writer Pico Iyer's description of Hong Kong has yet to be bettered. From opium port to Cold War enclave to frenetic financial capital, Hong Kong has never been boring. This is the hedonistic engine room of cultural fusion: East meets West in high style, and the results astonish and delight. Prepare to experience one of the most dramatic urban environments ever conceived.

1 The Peak
Take the tram to the lofty heights of Victoria Peak for an amazing view of the city *(see pp8–9).*

2 Statue Square
Hong Kong Island's northeast is the region's administrative centre. Colonial remnants and exciting modern architecture stand next to each other around Statue Square *(see pp10–11).*

3 Happy Valley Races
Horseracing below the high-rises: Happy Valley is where Hong Kongers go to play *(see pp12–13).*

Star Ferry 4
Ignore the subterranean road and rail links between Hong Kong Island and Kowloon. The thrilling way to cross the water is on the Star Ferry *(see pp14–15).*

Mai Po Marsh
Mai P
Yuen Long
Sha Po T
Kam Tin
Lam Tei
Yuen Kong
Yueng Siu Hang
Tai Lam Country Park
Tin Fu
Tuen Mun
Sham Tseng
Tsu
Tsing Shan Wan (Castle Peak Bay)
Shek Wan
Chek Lap Kok
Discovery Bay
Tung Chung
Lantau Island
Mui Wo
🔟 *Lantau Peak*
Cheung Sha
Shek Pik
Chimawan Peninsula
9 Cheung Chau Island
West Lamma

5 — miles ⌐ 0 ⌐ km — 5

Temple Street Night Market 6

Kowloon is at its most atmospheric at night. Head up the peninsula to the narrow lanes of Yau Ma Tei for some serious haggling (see pp18–19).

5 Stanley
An old fort steeped in colonial history and reminders of World War II, Stanley on the Southside of Hong Kong Island is a peaceful diversion from the frenetic city (see pp16–17).

Heritage Museum 7

Near Sha Tin in the New Territories, Hong Kong's best museum is a must. Splendid high-tech audio-visual displays cover the region's rich cultural heritage and natural history (see pp20–21).

Tai Long Wan 8 Coastline

The remote, rugged Sai Kung Peninsula in the New Territories is the place to find Hong Kong's finest beaches (see pp22–3).

9 Cheung Chau Island
Of the many islands around Hong Kong, tiny Cheung Chau is arguably the loveliest, with traces of old China (see pp24–5).

Big Buddha and Po Lin Monastery
10 In the middle of hilly Lantau Island, Po Lin Monastery is a major destination for devotees and tourists alike. The extraordinary seated Big Buddha image facing the monastery can be seen from miles away (see pp28–9).

The Peak

With Hong Kong's most spectacular views, cooler climes and quiet wooded walks, it's no wonder Victoria Peak is so popular with tourists and the super rich who occupy the exclusive properties clinging to its high slopes. The Peak Tram takes under 10 minutes to reach Victoria Gap, pinning you to your seat as it's hauled up the sheer slope at the end of a single cable (don't worry, its safety record is spotless).

Terrace dining

The Peak Tram

🕙 If the weather is misty or there's low cloud, put off a visit to the Peak until a clearer day as the chances are you'll be able to see very little.

🍽 In the Peak Tower, Café Deco's smart interior, wide food choices and good service make it an excellent drinking and dining stop. For fantastic sea views over to Lamma Island dine or drink in the Peak Lookout's lovely garden terrace.

• Map E5 • Peak Tram 7am–midnight daily
• Single/return HK$20/$30 • Bus 15C from Central Star Ferry
• 2849 7654
• www.thepeak.com.hk

Top 10 Sights

1. Peak Tower
2. Galleria
3. The Peak Lookout
4. Barker and Plantation Roads
5. Pok Fu Lam Country Park
6. World's Most Expensive House
7. Victoria Peak Garden
8. Old Peak Road
9. View near Summit
10. Lugard and Harlech Roads

Peak Tower

The Peak Tram empties into this ugly anvil-shaped mall *(below)* containing shops, cafés, restaurants and viewing gallery. The refreshment and tourist trinkets inside don't inspire, but children may enjoy the fantastical motion simulator Peak Explorer ride, Madame Tussaud's waxworks or the gruesome bric-à-brac in Ripley's Believe It Or Not Odditorium.

Galleria

Although the imposing Peak Tower mall is hardly sensitive to its grand setting there is a good range of places to eat and drink inside its Galleria, with great views down onto city and harbour, and across to Lamma Island.

The Peak Lookout

The new incarnation of this much-loved, up-market drinking and dining favourite retains a lovely garden terrace, great food and friendly ambience.

4 Barker and Plantation Roads

These usually quiet (although pavement-free) roads are worth wandering for a peep at some of the Peak's pricier properties, including 23 Severn Road (below). Most have amazing harbour views. But dream on. You would have to be a millionaire just to afford a two-bedroom flat here.

5 Pok Fu Lam Country Park

For a gentle half-hour ramble, head down Pok Fu Lam Reservoir Road, then catch a bus back into town.

9 View near Summit

The summit itself is fenced off and covered by telecom masts, but the views from the edges of Victoria Peak Garden are excellent *(above)*.

10 Lugard and Harlech Roads

The effortless way to see most of the best views on offer from the Peak is on the shaded, well-paved, 2-mile (3-km) circular walk along Lugard Road and Harlech Road. It also makes a terrific jogging track with a view.

6 World's Most Expensive House

In 1997 an offer of HK$900m for the newly built property at 23 Severn Road was incredibly refused. Weeks later, prices crashed, and by 2001 the house was valued at a "mere" third of the price.

8 Old Peak Rd

The old footpath up to the Peak before the Peak Tram arrived is pleasant and shaded. But the traffic can be busy at the bottom of Peak Road so it's best to detour onto Treginter Path near the bottom.

7 Victoria Peak Garden

The steep struggle up Mount Austin Road or the longer route along the Governor's Walk to these well-tended gardens *(right)* is worth the effort. The viewing platform faces Lamma Island.

The Peak Tram

Despite the fact that a single steel cable hauls the tram up a long and incredibly steep track, the Peak Tram has a faultless safety record since the service opened in 1888. The most severe disruption to services came in the 1960s when torrents of water from an especially violent typhoon washed part of the track away.

Central's Statue Square

Stand in Central district's Statue Square and you're right in the region's financial, political, historical and social heart. Among the steel and glass of sleek skyscrapers surrounding the square are a few colonial remnants, including the handsome Neo-Classical Legislation Council Building where Hong Kong's usually low-key political demonstrations take place. Shopping, a much more popular Hong Kong pursuit than politics, goes on inside the swanky boutiques opposite.

Thomas Jackson statue

Bank of China Tower

Top 10 Sights

1. Bank of China Tower
2. Shopping Malls
3. The Cenotaph
4. Chater Garden
5. Court of Appeal
6. The Legislative Council Building
7. Mandarin Oriental
8. Thomas Jackson Statue
9. HSBC Bank Headquarters
10. Sunday Filipino Fiesta

🕐 For a terrific bird's-eye view over Central and the harbour, head to the viewing gallery on the 47th floor of the Bank of China Tower.

🍴 If you fancy picnicking in the square or in nearby Chater Garden, try the fantastic pastries, cakes and quiches from the Mandarin Oriental's Cake Shop, which is at the edge of the square.

• Map L5

1 Bank of China Tower

Looming over the HSBC building is the imposing 70-storey Bank of China Tower. It was designed by the renowned architect I M Pei. The tower is a dizzying 368 m (1,207 ft) high. It doesn't please everyone – those who know about feng shui say it projects negative vibes onto other buildings.

2 Shopping Malls

Two of Hong Kong's most upmarket and, of course, pricey shopping malls – the busy Landmark Centre and the less busy Prince's Building *(see p63)* – sit next to Statue Square. Within these hallowed temples to conspicuous overspending are many of the city's most exclusive and elegant boutiques, including the likes of Armani, Gucci and Prada.

3 The Cenotaph

Standing at the northern edge of Statue Square, the Cenotaph *(left)* is a memorial to those who died in the two World Wars.

For more about Hong Kong's modern buildings **See pp42–3**

Chater Garden
4 Despite the prime real-estate value on the site of what used to be the old pitch of the Hong Kong Cricket Club, the small but well-tended Chater Garden *(below)* sprang up instead of a skyscraper. It's free to enter and makes a good place to enjoy a cold drink and rest tired legs.

Court of Final Appeal
5 Behind the HSBC building, a handsome 150-year-old redbrick building used to house a French Catholic mission and the old colony's first Government House. Today it serves as one of Hong Kong's courts of law.

HSBC Bank Headquarters
9 On its completion in 1985, Sir Norman Foster's bold building was the most expensive ever built, costing more than HK$5bn. The edifice is said to have the strongest feng shui in Hong Kong. Rubbing the paws of the bank's handsome lions *(above)* is said to bring good luck.

Sunday Filipino Fiesta
10 Hundreds of young Filipinos and Indonesians, mostly domestic workers enjoying their only day off, occupy almost every spare bit of public space in Central.

The Legislative Council Building
6 One of Hong Kong's last remaining colonial buildings, the elegant Neo-Classical Legislative Council building *(right)*, which used to house the Supreme Court, now serves as Hong Kong's parliament.

Mandarin Oriental
7 It's hard to believe, but the Mandarin Oriental was once Hong Kong's tallest building. Today its graceful exterior seems overwhelmed by the ceaseless traffic, but inside it's still one of Hong Kong's finest hotels.

Thomas Jackson Statue
8 Appropriately enough, one of Hong Kong's few remaining statues, of a 19th-century banker, is in Statue Square. The Japanese army removed one of Queen Victoria, which gave the square its name.

Suffocating Suffrage
During Handover negotiations *(see p31)*, China was adamant that Hong Kong's Legislative Council would be as democratic under Chinese rule as under the British (in other words, it could be argued, hardly at all). When Chris Patten, the last governor, tried introducing greater representation, China dubbed Patten, among other things, "a strutting prostitute" and "serpent".

For key moments in Hong Kong history See pp30–31

Happy Valley Races

Feel the earth move beneath thundering hooves as you cheer the finishers home in the ultimate Hong Kong night out. Races have been held at Happy Valley – the widest stretch of flat land on Hong Kong Island, originally a swamp – since 1846. Today the action takes place beneath twinkling high-rises making for one of the most atmospheric horseracing tracks in the world.

A winner

Pre-race parade

🌀 If you don't want to spend the whole evening at the races, arrive after the first few races have been run, when admission is free.

🅾 Moon Koon Restaurant (2966 7111), on the second floor of the main stand, offers good, reasonably priced food. Advance booking is required on race nights.

• Less than a mile (1 km) south of Causeway Bay and Wanchai on Hong Kong Island • Map P6
• Regular meetings Wed, Sat & Sun • Dial 1817 for race details • www.hongkongjockey club.com • Adm HK$10
• Racing Museum 2966 8065, free
• Come Horseracing Tour 2366 3995, HK$190–460

Top 10 Sights

1. Wednesday Night Races
2. The Big Screen
3. Racing Museum
4. View from Moon Koon
5. Come Horseracing Tour
6. Silver Lining Skeleton
7. The Crowd
8. Types of Bet
9. Where to Bet
10. Jockey Club Booths

1 Wednesday Night Races
The most exciting scheduled races are fortnightly on Wednesday evenings. For the full atmosphere, jump on a Happy Valley-bound tram and bone up on the form in the Wednesday *Racing Post* on the way. The first race is usually at 7:30pm.

2 The Big Screen
The huge screen facing the stand *(below)* carries all the statistics racegoers need from the results of the last race to odds on the upcoming one. There are also live race pictures or replays, ensuring no one misses any of the action.

3 Racing Museum
The small and neat museum at Happy Valley details Hong Kong's racing history along with a selection of Chinese art celebrating the horse. Learn the story of the old trade in prized Mongolian and Chinese ponies. Don't aim to combine it with an evening at the races, however. It is closed during meetings.

單T派彩
TRIO DIVIDEN
場大 RACE 3
1 - 2 - 1(
$ 469.00

4 View from Moon Koon

For a fantastic track-side view while you eat, head to the Moon Koon Restaurant. Racing and dining packages are available.

7 The Crowd

Happy Valley has a 55,000 capacity but is so popular that it sometimes sells out before the day. The enthusiasm among the big-betting, chain-smoking punters is infectious. Stand in the open next to the track where you'll get the full effect of the roar from the stands and a good view of the finishing line.

9 Where to Bet

Bets are placed at the counters at the back of each floor of the main stand. Pick up the right betting slips next to the counters, fill them in and take them to the counter with your stake money. If you win, wait for a few minutes after the race, then go to the same counter to collect your winnings.

5 Come Horse-racing Tour

Splendid Tours runs the Come Horseracing Tour held during scheduled race meetings on Wednesdays, Saturdays and Sundays. Tours include entry to the Members' Enclosure, welcome drink, buffet meal and guide service.

6 Silver Lining Skeleton

Silver Lining, Hong Kong's most famous horse, was the first to win more than HK$1m. The equine skeleton takes pride of place in a glass cabinet at the Racing Museum.

8 Types of Bet

Different ways to bet include simply guessing the winner; a place (betting your horse comes 1st or 2nd, or 1st, 2nd or 3rd if seven or more horses race); a quinella (picking 1st and 2nd in any order); and a quinella place (predicting any two of the first three horses in any order).

10 Jockey Club Booths

For help and advice on placing bets go to the friendly, helpful Jockey Club officials at the booths between the main entrance and the racetrack. The Jockey Club is the only organization allowed to take bets in Hong Kong. The tax it collects makes up a small but significant percentage of government revenue, but is being threatened by illegal and online betting. Jockey Club profits go to local charities.

Hong Kong's biggest payout

A world record total of US$92m was paid out at Happy Valley's sister track at Sha Tin in 1997. More than 350 bets of HK$1.30 each collected HK$260,000.

TOP 10 Star Ferry

One of Hong Kong's best-loved institutions, the Star Ferries have plied between Kowloon and Hong Kong Island since 1888. The portly green and white 1950s and 60s relics are still used by commuters despite the advent of rail and road tunnels beneath the harbour. A ferry ride offers a thrilling perspective on the towering skyscrapers and the jungle-clad hills of Hong Kong Island. Take an evening voyage for the harbour's neon spectacle, especially the elaborate light displays at Christmas.

Batwing junk

Crewmen, Star Ferry

🐾 The HKTB office in the Tsim Sha Tsui Star ferry building is the most convenient place to pick up brochures, get help and advice, and to buy Star Ferry models and other souvenirs.

☕ The Pacific Coffee Company inside the terminal serves a reasonable cup of coffee. Alternatively try the HK$10 fresh lemonade and free cookie samples from Mrs Fields.

• Map L5–M4 • Ferries 6:30am–11:30pm daily. Frequency varies from 5 to 10 minutes • www.starferry.com.hk • 2367 7065

Top 10 Sights

1. The Fleet
2. Clocktower
3. Star Ferry Crew
4. Star Ferry Routes
5. Skyline South
6. Victoria Harbour
7. Sightseeing Bargain
8. Ferry Decks
9. Ocean Terminal
10. Skyline North

1 The Fleet

In the early days, four coal-fired boats went back and forth between Hong Kong and Kowloon. Today 12 diesel-powered vessels operate, each named after a particular star (with the night-time glare and pollution, they may be the only stars you're likely to see from the harbour).

3 Star Ferry Crew

Many Star Ferry crew members still sport old-fashioned sailor-style uniforms, making popular subjects for camera-toting visitors. Watch out, too, for the pier crewmen catching the mooring rope with a long billhook.

2 Clocktower

Standing next to the Tsim Sha Tsui Star Ferry, the landmark clocktower is the last remnant of the old Kowloon railway terminus. This was the poetic final stop for trains from the mainland, including the Orient Express from London. The terminus has since moved east to prosaic Hung Hom.

4 Star Ferry Routes

The Star Ferries run four routes: between Tsim Sha Tsui and Central; Tsim Sha Tsui and Wanchai; Central and Hung Hom; and Hung Hom and Wanchai.

6 Victoria Harbour

Victoria harbour is the busiest stretch of water in Hong Kong, teeming with activity. Keep your eyes peeled at the weekend for the last remaining batwing sailing junk to be found in this part of China.

8 Ferry Decks

The lower and upper decks used to be first (upper) and second (lower) class compartments. Today the extra cents buy access to the air-conditioning section during the hottest months, and afford a better view of the city and refuge from sea spray on choppy days.

9 Ocean Terminal

Just north of the Tsim Sha Tsui terminal, Hong Kong's cruise ships dock, including, on occasion, the QE2. Some US warships also dock here during port calls.

10 Skyline North

As you approach Kowloon with Hong Kong Island behind you, you'll see the Arts and Cultural Centre, closest to the shore. Behind it rises the grand, modern extension of the Peninsula Hotel topped by its twin helipads. The craggy hills of the New Territories loom in the background.

5 Skyline South

As you cross Victoria Harbour, on the far left are the glass and flowing lines of the Convention Centre *(right)* in Wanchai and above it the 373-m (1,223-ft) tower of Central Plaza. Further left are the Bank of China's striking zig-zags, and the struts and spars of the HSBC building. The new kid on the block is Two International Finance Centre *(see pp42–3)*, the island's tallest skyscraper, towering a colossal 420 m (1,378 ft) above Star Ferry Pier.

7 Sightseeing Bargain

At HK$1.7 to ride on the lower deck and HK$2.2 to ride the top deck, the Star Ferry is Hong Kong's best sightseeing bargain.

For more ways to get around Hong Kong **See p138**

Top 10 Stanley

Originally a sleepy fishing haven, Stanley was the largest settlement on Hong Kong Island before the British moved in. The modern town, hugging the southern coast, still makes a peaceful, pleasant escape from the bustle of the city. Traffic is minimal, and the pace of life relaxed, with plenty of excellent places to eat, good beaches and a large market to search for clothes, silks and souvenirs. Stanley is also the place to glimpse colonial Hong Kong and an older Chinese tradition seen at the Tin Hau Temple.

Stanley market

Murray Building

🕐 If you hate crowds, avoid Stanley at weekends when the town and market become very busy and the buses to and from Central fill up.

Sit at the front of the top deck of the bus to fully appreciate the dramatic coast road out to Stanley.

🍴 For great al fresco dining, El Cid in the Murray building offers good tapas and the best views *(see p77)*.

• Map F6 • Buses 6, 6A, 6X or 260 from Central • Stanley market 9am–6pm daily

Top 10 Sights

1. Market
2. Murray House
3. Old Police Station
4. Waterfront
5. Stanley Beach
6. Tin Hau Temple
7. War Cemetery
8. Stanley Fort
9. St Stephen's Beach
10. Pubs and Restaurants

Market
1 Reasonably priced clothes, shoes and accessories as well as plenty of tourist tat are to be found among Stanley's pleasant, ramshackle market stalls. Although it's not the cheapest or best market in Hong Kong, you may as well potter among the hundred or so stalls before heading to a café or one of the seafront eateries.

Murray House
2 This venerable Neo-Classical relic dating from 1843, originally served as British Army quarters on the site now occupied by the Bank of China Tower in Central *(see p10)*. It was dismantled and reassembled here and now houses a number of restaurants *(right)*.

Old Police Station
3 The handsome building was built in 1859 and is Hong Kong's oldest surviving police station building. The Japanese used it as a headquarters during World War II. Today it houses a restaurant.

4 Waterfront

The pretty waterfront makes a pleasant promenade between the market area and Murray House. The harbour was once home to a busy fleet of junks and fishing boats, but is now empty.

5 Stanley Beach

This fine stretch of sand is perfect for a dip and a paddle. It's the venue for the fiercely contested dragon boat races in June when the beach fills with competitors and revellers.

6 Tin Hau Temple

Lined with the grimacing statues of guards to the sea goddess Tin Hau, the gloomy interior of this temple is one of the most evocative in Hong Kong. It's also one of the oldest Tin Hau temples in the region, dating back to 1767.

7 War Cemetery

Most of the graves are the resting place of residents who died during World War II. Others date back to early colonial days, when many settlers, young and old, succumbed to a range of tropical illnesses.

8 Stanley Fort

The old British army barracks at the end of the peninsula is now occupied by the Chinese People's Liberation Army (closed to public).

9 St Stephen's Beach

Another good stretch of sand, St Stephen's is also the place for sailing and canoeing. The small pier is the departure point for the Sunday boat bound for the remote island of Po Toi (see p114).

10 Pubs and Restaurants

One of Stanley's best attractions is its excellent range of restaurants and bars (see p77). A host of eateries, from Italian to Vietnamese, are lined along Stanley Main Road, facing the sea, many with outdoor seating. Murray House also contains good restaurants.

The War Dead

After Japan overran Hong Kong in 1941 (see p74), captured civilians suffered for three years under a regime of neglect, starvation and torture. The remains of thousands of servicemen and civilians who died here during the war are buried at Stanley cemetery.

10 Temple Street Night Market

Beneath the bleaching glare of a thousand naked light bulbs, tourists and locals alike pick their way among the stalls crowding the narrow lanes of Yau Ma Tei's Temple Street. The overwhelming array of cheap goods includes clothes, shoes, accessories, designer fakes, copy CDs, bric-a-brac and a generous helping of junk. Prices here may be a bit higher than in Shenzhen, just over the Chinese border or in some of Hong Kong's less well-known markets, but Temple Street is unbeatable for atmosphere.

Silk jacket

Browsing shoppers

🌀 A good way to tackle the night market is to start at the top by taking the MTR to Yau Ma Tei and walk south from Portland Street. This way you'll end up closer to the restaurants, hotels and bars of Tsim Sha Tsui when you've finished shopping.

🍽 Snack at the *dai pai dongs* (street stalls).

• Map M1–2 • The market gets going after 7pm and goes on until as late as 11pm

Top 10 Sights

1. Fortune Tellers
2. Canto Opera Street Performers
3. Dai Pai Dongs
4. Reclamation St Canteens
5. Best Watches
6. Best Clothes
7. Best Leather Goods
8. Best Shoes
9. Best Accessories
10. Best Knick-knacks

1 Fortune Tellers

A dozen fortune tellers operate around the junction of Temple and Market streets. Most are face and palm readers. The caged white finches are trained to pick a fortune card from the pack in return for some seeds.

2 Canto Opera Street Performers

On some evenings musicians and singers perform popular Cantonese Opera numbers next door to the fortune tellers.

3 Dai Pai Dongs

Tighter health regulations have made *dai pai dong* food stalls a rare sight, but they are alive and well at Temple Street, selling a variety of Chinese snacks, savoury pancakes, fishballs, seafood kebabs and unspecified meat offerings.

For more markets See pp38–9

4 Reclamation St Canteens

If you haven't had your fill from the *dai pai dongs*, try the cheap noodles and rice-based food at the covered stalls on Reclamation Street. Don't mind your neighbour's table manners, it's the done thing to drop or spit gristle and bone onto the table-tops here.

6 Best Clothes

Amid the naff and poly-fabric horrors (beware naked flames), good buys include cheap t-shirts, elaborate silks, beaded tops and cotton dresses. Have a look at the stall on the corner of Kansu St. Further down, tailored trousers can be ordered with a four-day turnaround.

7 Best Leather Goods

Leather is not really Temple Street's strong point. But belts are cheap, and there are plenty of leather handbags and shoulder bags, including fake Gucci, Elle and Burberry items. Some are more convincing than others.

8 Best Shoes

From the very cheap flip flops to the reasonable suede or leather shoes, bargain footwear is available almost everywhere on Temple Street, although the variety is not huge and the styles not that elegant. Don't forget to check the shops behind the stalls. A few stalls sell designer fakes.

Best Watches 5

It's likely to be a decent timekeeper but with no guarantees. The local makes and Western fakes are usually good value for money. One stall offers genuine, secondhand watches.

Haggling

Remember, prices given are mostly starting points and the mark-ups are significant. The merchandise here is far cheaper in China, so haggle hard (but do it with a smile), and remember the vendor is making a profit whatever price you both agree on. Begin below half the asking price and you should be able to knock up to 50% off some of the bigger ticket items.

9 Best Accessories

Cheap sunglasses are easy to find in the market. Embroidered and beaded handbags and shoulder bags are also worth looking out for.

10 Best Knick-knacks

Mao memorabilia, old posters, coins, opium pipes and jade are found on Public Square Street. Temple Street's northern extremity is rich in kitsch plastic Japanese cartoon merchandise, including Hello Kitty clocks, Afro Ken and Pokémon.

TOP 10 Heritage Museum

Hong Kong's newest museum, on the outskirts of Sha Tin in the New Territories, is by far its best (although the revamped History Museum in Kowloon is also worth a visit). Opened in 2000, the Heritage Museum covers the culture, arts and natural history of Hong Kong and the New Territories. Exciting audio-visual exhibits and a good interactive section for children make for a fun day out.

Photograph of Tai O in 1966

Museum entrance

🏇 Combine a visit to the museum with a trip to the races at Sha Tin if you can *(see p101)*.

Admission to the Heritage Museum is free on Wednesdays.

🍴 There is a small café and gift shop in the lobby.

• Map E3 • 1 Man Lam Road, Sha Tin, New Territories • 2180 8188
• Free shuttle bus from Sha Tin KCR
• www.heritage museum.gov.hk
• 10am–6pm Mon, Wed–Sat, 10am–7pm Sun & public hols
• Adm HK$10

Top 10 Features

1. Architecture and Design
2. Orientation Theatre
3. Children's Discovery Gallery
4. Cantonese Opera Hall
5. Thematic Exhibitions
6. Chao Shao-an Gallery
7. Courtyard
8. New Territories Culture
9. New Territories History
10. T T Tsui Gallery

1 Architecture and Design

The Heritage Museum building is based on the traditional Chinese *si he yuan* style, built around a courtyard. The style is still visible in the walled villages of the New Territories *(see p104)*.

3 Children's Discovery Gallery

The brightly coloured gallery is a vibrant, fun way to introduce children to local nature and archaeology, and the history of toys. Interactive exhibits and the child-size 3-D models are very popular with young children.

2 Orientation Theatre

For a brief overview of the museum, visit the Orientation Theatre on the ground floor opposite the ticket office. A short film in English and Cantonese (in rotation) explains the exhibits and the main aims of the museum.

Key

▨	Ground floor
▨	1st floor
▨	2nd floor

4 Cantonese Opera Hall

Cantonese opera is an obscure subject. However, the sumptuous costumes, intricate stage sets and snatches of song from the elaborate operas of Guangdong and Guanxi go some way to illustrating the attraction.

5 Thematic Exhibitions

Five halls on the first and second floors house temporary exhibitions focusing on subjects varying from popular culture, contemporary art and social issues in Hong Kong, to traditional Chinese art and history.

6 Chao Shao-an Gallery

The delicate ink on scroll paintings of artist and one-time Hong Kong resident Chao Shao-An are known far beyond China. There are dozens of fine examples in the gallery *(left)*.

7 Courtyard

For fresh air and interesting surroundings, head to the shaded courtyard *(above)* in the centre of the complex.

8 New Territories Culture

Large mock-ups of old maritime and village scenes *(below)* recreate the pre-colonial days. The growth of the new towns, such as Sha Tin, are also covered.

9 New Territories History

The rich fauna and flora of the region are exhibited along with 6000-year-old artifacts from the early days of human habitation in Hong Kong.

10 TT Tsui Gallery

The works of art dating from Neolithic times to the 20th century include porcelain, bronze, jade and stone artifacts, furniture, laquerware and Tibetan religious statues.

Hong Kong's Earliest Settlers

The New Territories History hall tells the scant story of Hong Kong's original inhabitants. Bronze Age people left behind axe and arrowheads in various parts of the territory more than 4,000 years ago, along with some mysterious rock carvings. Excavations on Lamma Island have turned up artifacts from an older Stone Age civilisation, dating back about 6,000 years.

ᴛᴼᴾ10 Tai Long Wan Coastline

Although only a few miles from urban Hong Kong, the remote, pristine beaches on the eastern edge of the rugged Sai Kung Peninsula seem like another country. There is no rail link and few roads, so you will have to make an early start, taking a bus to Sai Kung town, another bus to Pak Tam Au, then walk the hilly 4-mile (6-km) footpath to the beach. Alternatively, hire a junk. The reward for your effort will be glorious surf, delightful hidden pools and shaded cafés.

Bridge from Ham Tin village

Ham Tin beach

🍃 Buy the HKTB's *Sai Kung Explorer's Guide* for its detailed map and information.

🍴 The only eating options are beach cafés, or you can stock up for a picnic at Sai Kung town.

• Map G3 • Take the frequent 92 bus from Diamond Hill KCR terminating at Sai Kung town, then the half-hourly 94 bus (or 96R on Sun) to Pak Tam Au. Allow about 90 minutes from Kowloon or Central to the start of the path, plus at least an hour each way to hike to and from the beach
• Daily junk hire from HK$3000, see Yellow Pages for listings

Top 10 Sights

1. Beaches
2. Natural Swimming Pools
3. Beach Cafés
4. Ham Tin to Tai Long Path
5. Surf Action
6. Pleasure Junks
7. Hakka Fisherfolk
8. Campsite
9. Sharp Peak
10. Ham Tin Bridge

1 Beaches
There are three excellent beaches at Tai Long Wan. Tai Wan is the most remote and unspoiled; the smallest beach, Ham Tin, has a good café and camping area; Tai Long Sai Wan is the busiest.

2 Natural Swimming Pools
A lovely series of waterfalls and natural swimming pools *(left)* is the area's best-kept secret. Reach them from the path running alongside the small river at the northwestern end of Tai Long Sai Wan beach.

3 Beach Cafés
Noodles, fried rice and hot and cold drinks are available from the modest, reasonably priced cafés on Tai Long Sai Wan and the Hoi Fung café at Ham Tin.

4 Ham Tin to Tai Long Path

Take the steep half-mile (1-km) path between Ham Tin and Tai Long Sai Wan for lovely views down onto Ham Tin, Tai Wan and the mountains behind.

5 Surf Action

Tai Wan usually has reasonably good surf. Gentle body-boarding should always be possible, and you may even be able to surf properly when storms raise bigger swells.

6 Pleasure Junks

Most privately hired junks drop anchor at Tai Long Sai Wan, and their passengers head to the beach in smaller craft, making this the busiest of the three beaches.

8 Campsite

The area just east of Ham Tin village is the best place for overnight campers (right), with flat ground, public toilets and a stream for fresh water. There are no hotels.

9 Sharp Peak

The prominent 468-m (1,497-ft) summit of Sharp Peak is clearly visible from Ham Tin and Tai Wan. The arduous climb up its very steep slopes rewards with spectacular views over the peninsula.

10 Ham Tin Bridge

If you want to keep your feet dry, the only way onto the beach from Ham Tin village is via a rickety bridge. Marvel at the makeshift engineering from nailed-together driftwood and offcuts.

7 Hakka Fisherfolk

Tai Long village *(above)* may have been first settled in prehistoric times. It was a thriving Hakka fishing village until the 1950s, when most people migrated to the city or abroad. A few elderly residents remain.

The Route Out

A good route out of Tai Long Wan is the lovely, scenic path heading southwest from Sai Wan village, winding in gentle gradients around the edge of High Island Reservoir. Once you hit the main road outside Pak Tam Chung, you've a good chance of picking up a bus or taxi back into Sai Kung town.

TOP 10 Cheung Chau Island

This tiny, charming island, a half-hour ferry ride west of Hong Kong, makes a great escape from the heat and hassles of the city, except maybe at weekends when everyone else has the same idea. The sense of an older, traditional Hong Kong is pervasive among the narrow streets, tiny shops and temples of this old pirate and fishing haven. It's possible to see most of the island in a day, and there are some lovely secluded walks. The seafood is cheap and there are small but excellent stretches of beach.

Lion, Pak Tai Temple

Cheung Chau harbour

🚲 To really nip around the island, hire a bicycle from opposite the basketball courts close to Pak Tai Temple.

Look out for Cheung Chau's miniature fire engine and ambulance *(see p116)*.

🍴 If you've had your fill of seafood, try Morocco's (2986 9767), by the ferry pier, which serves decent Indian, Thai and Western (but not Moroccan) fare in the evenings.

• Map C6 • Daily ferries hourly or half-hourly from Outlying Islands ferry piers

Top 10 Sights

1. Pak Tai Temple
2. Harbour
3. Venerable Banyan Tree
4. Tung Wan Beach
5. "The Peak"
6. Pirates Cave
7. Windsurfing Centre
8. Boatbuilding Yard
9. Seafood Restaurants
10. Ancient Rock Carvings

1 Pak Tai Temple

This recently renovated temple is dedicated to Pak Tai, Cheung Chau's patron deity who is credited with saving islanders from plague. The temple is the centre for the annual bun festival celebrations *(see p36)*, when mounds of buns are piled up to be offered to resident ghosts. The festival dates from the time of plagues in the 19th century, which were considered to be the vengeance of those killed by local pirates.

2 Harbour

Although Hong Kong's fishing industry has dwindled from its heyday, plenty of commercial fishing boats still operate from Cheung Chau's typhoon shelter. Cheap cycle hire is available along the waterfront.

3 Venerable Banyan Tree

On Tung Wan Road is a tree *(below)* that is thought to be the source of Cheung Chau's good fortune. It is so revered by islanders that in recent years a restaurant opposite was knocked down instead of the tree to make way for a road extension.

For more about Cheung Chau's bun festival See p36

4 Tung Wan Beach

The island's finest beach is on the east coast, 150 m (500 ft) from the west coast's ferry pier *(above)*. It is tended by lifeguards and has a shark net.

5 "The Peak"

A walk up the hill along Don Bosco and Peak roads will take you past some lovely old colonial houses and beautiful sea views. The cemetery on Peak Road has especially fine vistas.

6 Pirates Cave

The place where a 19th-century buccaneer Cheung Po-Tsai supposedly stashed his booty, this "cave" is more of a hole or crevice. Take a torch to explore. The sea views nearby are lovely.

7 Windsurfing Centre

The family of Olympic gold-medalist Lee Lai-Shan operates the windsurfing centre and café near Tung Wan.

8 Boatbuilding Yard

At the harbour's northern end is a busy yard where junks are built and nets mended. Look out for the slabs of ice sliding along the overhead chute, down a mini-helter-skelter and onto the boats.

9 Seafood Restaurants

If you want to dine on fish or shellfish, there's plenty of choice along the seafront on She Praya Road north and south of the ferry pier. The restaurants are cheaper than other seafood centres such as Lamma. Choose from the live tanks *(above)*.

10 Ancient Rock Carving

In the Hong Kong region are several rock carvings in close proximity to the sea. Cheung Chau has one facing the sea just below the Warwick Hotel. Nothing is known of the people who carved these shapes about 3,000 years ago.

Paths and Walks

A footpath weaves around the southern edge of the island, taking in clifftop walks and a small Tin Hau Temple at the tiny Moring Beach. Heading southwest from here will take you along Peak Road past the cemetery to Sai Wan's small harbour. From here you can take a sampan shuttle back to the ferry pier at Cheung Chau village.

 Following pages **The Big Buddha at Po Lin, Lantau**

🔟 Big Buddha and Po Lin Monastery

Once a humble house built by three monks to worship Buddha, Po Lin Monastery on Lantau Island is now a large and important temple. Its crowning glory, the giant Buddha statue facing the monastery, is an object of veneration for devotees and one of Hong Kong's most popular tourist sights. The statue dominates the area from a plinth reached by more than 260 steps. On a clear day, the view across the valleys, reservoirs and peaks of Lantau makes the climb worthwhile.

Main courtyard

View of the Big Buddha

🌀 If you can face an early start, stay overnight at the Hong Kong Bank Foundation S G Davis Hostel (2985 5610) close to the Tea Gardens and rise before dawn to see the sunrise from the summit of nearby Lantau Peak.

🚫 If you don't fancy the cheap vegetarian food available inside the temple, take a picnic and wander the nearby footpaths for a good spot.

• Map B5 • No. 2 bus from Lantau Island's Mui Wo ferry terminal
• Monastery: 8am–6pm daily; Big Buddha:10am–5:30pm daily • Free

Top 10 Sights

1. The Big Buddha
2. Monastery
3. Tea Gardens
4. Vegetarian Restaurants
5. Great Hall
6. Bodhisattvas
7. Relic Inside the Buddha
8. Footpath Down to Tung Chung
9. Monks and Nuns
10. Temple Gateway

1 The Big Buddha

Standing a lofty 26 m (85 ft) high, this mighty bronze statue is among the largest seated Buddha images in the world. The statue, which was cast in more than 220 pieces, sits on a throne of lotus – the Buddhist symbol of purity.

2 Monastery

Attracted by its seclusion, Buddhist monks began arriving on Lantau in the early 20th century. The Po Lin or "precious lotus" monastery really developed as a place for pilgrimage in the 1920s when the Great Hall was built and the first abbot appointed.

3 Tea Gardens

The Tea Gardens just west of the Buddha statue boast their own modest tea plantation. The café sells tea leaves from the bushes and makes a pleasant shaded place to enjoy a drink or cheap Chinese meal away from the crowds.

For other sights on Lantau See pp112–17

Great Hall
5 The main temple houses three large golden Buddha images. Don't miss the ceiling paintings, the elaborate friezes around the exterior and the elegant lotus-shaped floor tiles.

Ngong Ping

TUNG CHUNG FORT
PO LIN MONASTERY **2**
S. G. DAVIS YOUTH HOSTEL
8
LANTAU TEA GARDENS
BUDDHA STATUE **1** **3**
LANTAU TRAIL
Lantau Peak
Tai O
Shek Pik Reservoir
FERRY TERMINAL

Vegetarian Restaurants
4 Meal tickets for three good-value restaurants are sold at the entrance to the Buddha statue (they also allow access to the displays inside the Buddha). The vegetarian food includes convincing mock meat dishes.

Bodhisattvas
6 On each side of the staircase are statues of Buddhist saints. They are venerated for deferring heaven in order to help mortals reach enlightenment. Throw a coin into their cupped hands for luck.

Relic Inside the Buddha
7 A sacred relic of the real Buddha (a tooth in a crystal container) is enshrined within the Buddha image, but is difficult to make out. Below the statue is a display about the life of the Buddha and his path to enlightenment.

Footpath Down to Tung Chung
8 Walk back down to Tung Chung MTR via the lovely 4-mile (7-km) wooded path through the Tung Chung Valley. You will pass some small monasteries including Lo Hon, which serves cheap vegetarian lunches.

Monks and Nuns
9 You may glimpse the grey-robed, shaven-headed nuns and monks at prayers in the old temple behind the main one. Entry is forbidden to tourists during the 3pm prayers.

Temple Gateway
10 Guarded by twin lions, the temple gateway is said to replicate the southern gate to Buddhist heaven. As found elsewhere in the temple, the

gateway is decorated with reverse swastikas, which is the holy sign of Buddhism. The three Chinese characters at the top read "Po Lin Monastery".

Falun Gong at the Big Buddha

In 2000, during an official meeting on the mainland, Po Lin's abbot spoke out against the Falun Gong, the semi-religious sect that's outlawed and repressed in China. As a result, local members of the so-called "evil cult" held a big demonstration near the Big Buddha, protesting that their promotion of physical and spiritual health through tai-chi style exercises is not evil.

Left **Colonial view** Centre **Chinese refugees at border, 1950** Right **Last governor, Chris Patten**

🔟 Moments in History

1 4000 BC: Early Peoples

For many years, the popular version of history was that Hong Kong was a "barren rock" devoid of people when the British arrived. In fact, archaeology now shows that scattered primitive clans had settled by the seaside on Hong Kong Island and the New Territories six millennia ago. Their diet was not politically correct by today's standards: bone fragments show they liked to eat dolphin.

19th-century pirate

2 AD 1127: Local Clans

When marauding Mongols drive the Song dynasty emperor's family out of the imperial capital of Kaifeng, one princess escapes to the walled village of Kam Tin in the New Territories, where she marries into the powerful Tang clan.

3 1841: The British Take Hong Kong Island

In a decisive move during the First Opium War between China and Britain, Captain Charles Elliot of the British Royal Navy lands on Hong Kong Island and plants the Union Jack on January 25. The 8,000-odd locals seem to take it in their stride, but China and Britain continue to fight over other Chinese trading cities. The 1842 Treaty of Nanking cedes Hong Kong Island to Britain.

4 1860: Land Claim

The good times are rolling in Hong Kong, where the population has now swelled to more than 86,000. The island is becoming cramped, however, and after a series of further skirmishes between Britain and China, the Kowloon Peninsula and Stonecutter's Island are ceded to Britain.

5 1898: The 99-Year Lease

Britain digs in, turning Hong Kong into a mighty fort. Lyemun at the eastern end of the island bristles with guns and the world's first wire-guided torpedo. Breathing space and water supplies are assured when on July 1, the 99-year lease of the New Territories is signed in Peking.

6 1941: Japanese Occupation

Hong Kong has guns galore defending the sea, but the Japanese

Left **Japanese soldiers captured by the British, 1945** Right **View of downtown Hong Kong, 1950s**

Chinese soldiers, morning after Handover

come by land. They have little trouble breaching the aptly named Gin Drinkers Line – a motley string of pillboxes. Hong Kong is surrendered two days before Christmas, beginning a brutal three-year occupation.

1950: Economic Miracle
7 The territory's economic miracle begins to unfold, as incoming refugees from China provide an eager workforce, and British rule keeps things on an even keel. Hong Kong's transformation into a manufacturing centre begins.

1984: Handover Agreed
8 The Sino-British Joint Declaration is promulgated, after years of secret talks between Margaret Thatcher and Deng Xiaoping. Deng coins the phrase "one country, two systems" to quell fears.

1997: Handover
9 Handover night on 30 June is widely regarded as an anticlimax after years of anticipation. The media focuses on soggy Union Jacks, last governor Chris Patten's tears, Prince Charles and his yacht, and Jiang Zemin's triumphant toast. The following dawn sees armoured cars rolling across the border.

1998: Financial Crisis
10 Asia's economic "tigers" are humbled as years of living on borrowed money finally take their toll. Hong Kong is not as badly hit as some countries, but the financial crisis bites nonetheless.

Top 10 Movers and Shakers

1 Jorge Alvares
In 1513 the Portuguese navigator Alvares becomes the first European to visit Hong Kong.

2 Cheung Po-Tsai
The Lantau-based pirate king Cheung Po-Tsai wreaks havoc with international traders in 1810.

3 Lin Tse Hsu
Commissioner Lin Tse Hsu is appointed by China in 1839, with the task of ending the trade in imported opium.

4 Captain Charles Elliot
Flag-planter Captain Charles Elliot claims Hong Kong Island for Britain in 1841.

5 Sir Henry Pottinger
Pottinger becomes Hong Kong's first governor. He turns a blind eye to illicit shipments of opium.

6 Dr Sun Yat-Sen
The reformer blasts China as "chaotic and corrupt" during a lecture at Hong Kong University in 1923. Economic boycott of the colony follows.

7 Rensuke Isogai
In 1941 the military commander begins his barbaric reign as Japan's wartime governor of Hong Kong.

8 Deng Xiaoping
The Chinese premier sticks to his principles during Handover talks in 1984.

9 Chris Patten
Lachrymose last governor Chris Patten waves goodbye to Hong Kong in 1997.

10 Tung Chee-Hwa
The shipping magnate Tung Chee-Hwa takes Hong Kong's helm after Handover.

Left **Traditional tonics** Centre **Junk** Right **Tai chi**

Ways to Experience the Real China

1 Spend a Night at the Opera

Cantonese opera might sound like discordant screeching to the untrained ear, but make no mistake, this is a fine and ancient art. It combines song, mime, dancing, martial arts and fantastic costumes and make-up and can go on for six hours or more. Call the HKTB (see p139) for details of performances.

Operatic figures

2 Ride on a Junk

We've all seen that iconic image of the junk, blood-red bat-wing sails unfurled as the sun sets over Victoria Harbour. Unfortunately, it's usually the same boat. *The Duk Ling* is one of the few masted sailing junks left. Trips can be organized through the HKTB. If you're wadded, you can hire one of the gin palaces masquerading as junks for around HK$5,000 a day. Check the classified pages in the *South China Morning Post*.

3 Feast on Dim Sum

Dim sum literally translates as "touch the heart", although in some establishments it may also touch your wallet. The small steamed snacks in bamboo baskets are delivered by grumpy old ladies with trolleys.

Dim sum

4 Visit a Market

Hong Kong's wet markets can bring on instant culture shock fo those tourists who are more used to the orderly atmosphere of supermarkets. Tiptoe through rivers of blood, past gizzards and buzzing flies as hawkers yel and housewives bargair

5 Go for a Traditional Tonic

For a taste of the real China, try a tonic restaurant. Chefs whip up dishes with all sorts of herbs spices and dangly bits, in accordance with the principles c "heating" or "cooling" foods. A tonic lunch at the Treasure Inn Seafood Restaurant includes fried snowfrog and bamboo fungi. ◎ 2/F Western Market, 323 Des Voeux Rd, Sheung Wan • Map J4 • 2850 7780 • $$

6 Try Foot Reflexology

Vice-like hands seek ou pressure points linked to vital organs. The procedure is painful, and you might be embarrassed about you feet, but you will feel so good when they stop. Reflexologists abound in Happy Valley Try On Wo Tong. ◎ 1/F Lai Shing Bldg, 13–19 Sing Woo Rd • 2893 0199

For 10 favourite dim sum appetizers See p51

Left **Chinese New Year** Right **Market produce**

7 Aim for Everything Zen

For a modern take on ancient China, check out the Chi Lin Nunnery in Kowloon. This gorgeous replica of a seven-hall Tang Dynasty (AD 618–907) complex took 10 years to build, using traditional techniques and materials. Bliss out as stubble-headed nuns chant to the Sakyamuni Buddha *(see p96).*

8 Experience Unbelievable Gall

She Wong Lam in the northeast of Hong Kong Island is the place to sup on snake wine, a traditional winter tonic. The speciality is a fiery brew containing the gall bladders of five deadly snakes. ⊗ *Hillier St, Sheung Wan • Map K5 • 2543 8032*

9 Watch a Lion Dance

Lions are thought to ward off evil and bring luck, which explains why the opening of a new building often features a troupe of wiry youths prancing about beneath a stylised lion's head. Common around Chinese New Year *(see p36).*

10 Practise Tai Chi

Turn up at the clocktower *(see p83)* near the Star Ferry in Tsim Sha Tsui at 8am on Tuesdays and Wednesdays, and you can enjoy an hour's free instruction in this gentlest of martial arts. ⊗ *Map M4*

Top 10 Ways to Pamper Yourself

1 Spa-ing Bout
Check into the Peninsula for a stress-busting two-day Spa Retreat. ⊗ *2920 2888*

2 Rubbed the Right Way
Go for a deep-tissue Chinese massage and get the blood circulating. ⊗ *On Wo Tong (see Reflexology entry)*

3 Breath of Fresh Air
Beat the pollution and enjoy the buzz at Oxyvital's Central "oxygen bar".

4 In a Lather
A hot shave from the Mandarin Oriental's Shanghai barber will leave your face feeling like a baby's bottom. ⊗ *2522 0111*

5 Love Potion No. 9
Boost your staying power with a tonic drink from one of the many kerbside Chinese medicine shops.

6 Geomancing the Stone
Make sure your house and garden are in tune with the elements with a private feng shui consultation. ⊗ *Raymond Lo 2736 9568*

7 Pins and Needles
Loosen up with an acupuncture session. ⊗ *On Wo Tong (see Reflexology entry)*

8 Masked Ball
Lie back for a facial at Jurlique, Kowloon Hotel basement. ⊗ *2368 3500*

9 Put Your Feet Up
Fans rave about the traditional Shanghai pedicure at the Mandarin Oriental. ⊗ *2522 0111*

10 The Doctor Is In
Try some alternative medicine from a traditional Chinese doctor. ⊗ *Dr Troy Sing 2526 7908*

For Hong Kong's best markets See pp38–9

Left **Chinese fisherman** Right **Schoolgirls**

Peoples and Cultures in Hong Kong

Chinese chequers

1 Chinese
With a history of revolution, migration, organized crime and incessant trading, the witty and streetwise Cantonese are the New Yorkers of China, and make up the majority of Hong Kong's population. There are migrant communities from every Chinese region, most notably the Shanghainese, Hakka and Chiu Chow.

2 British
Colonial power may have vanished, but a large British population remains, including a small but influential community of native-born. Influences are everywhere, from street names ("Lambeth Walk", "Rutland Quadrant") to school blazers.

3 Eurasian
The traditional role of this community of mixed European and Asian descent – as cultural and commercial brokers between East and West – remains undiminished. If anyone can claim to truly embody Hong Kong's intriguing duality, it is this young, wealthy and internationally-minded community.

4 Portuguese
In the Pearl River Delta since the arrival of traders in the 16th century, the Portuguese have inter-married extensively with the Cantonese. Aside from a clutch of surnames (da Silva, Sequeira, Remedios), a lasting influence has been the fostering of an addiction to egg tarts and pastries.

5 Indian
The history of Hong Kong's substantial Indian population (there are Hindus, Muslims and Sikhs) dates from the arrival of the British in 1841. Like the Eurasians, young Indians have rejected purely Western or Asian notions of identity, pioneering instead a synthesis of both.

6 Jewish
Hong Kong has one of the oldest Jewish communities in east Asia, producing patrician business dynasties (the Sassoons, the Kadoories) and one of the most colourful colonial governors (Sir Matthew Nathan, 1903–1906).

Street scene

Indian residents, Victoria Peak

Top 10 Patois and Lingo in Hong Kong

1 Chinglish
The local patois, which freely uses sinocized English words like *sahmunjee* (sandwich), *bahsee* (bus), *lumbah* (number) and *kayleem* (cream).

2 Portuguese
Many borrowings, including *praya* (waterfront road), *joss* (a corruption of *deus*, or god) and *amah* (maid).

3 Anglo-Indian/Persian
Several words, including *shroff* (cashier), *nullah* (channel or watercourse) and *tiffin* (lunch).

4 Mo Lei Tau
The impenetrable slang used by young Cantonese. Based on surreal and seemingly nonsensical phrasing.

5 "Jaihng"
All-purpose slang term meaning "cool", "excellent". (As used in the Hollywood film *Wayne's World*.)

6 "Yau Mehr Liu?"
Translates roughly as "What's your talent?" but used as a streetwise greeting; a bit like "what's up?" or "*wassup?*"

7 "Godown"
Hong Kong English for warehouse or storage facility; a contraction of "go put your load down".

8 "Whiskey Tangos"
Hong Kong police slang for "white trash".

9 "Aiyah!"
The universal exclamation of disappointment, surprise or regret.

10 "Ah-"
Prefix added to names when denoting affection, as in "Ah-Timothy", "Ah-Belinda".

7 Russian
A few now elderly descendants are all that is left of the former émigré community. Hong Kong's White Russians were once numerous, and you still find borsch on the menu of every takeaway and coffee shop.

8 Overseas Chinese
The surging growth in British-, American- and Canadian-born Chinese (nicknamed BBCs, ABCs and CBCs respectively) has been a characteristic of the last two decades, as the well-educated children of emigrants return in search of roots and white-collar work.

9 Filipino
Most members of the largest ethnic minority stoically perform the low-paid occupations that Hong Kongers shun, working as domestic servants, drivers, waiting staff and bar room musicians, and remitting most of their income back home to the Philippines. Filipinas promenade in their thousands every Sunday at Statue Square (see p11).

10 Australian
Working mostly in business and the media, the size of this community is reflected in the fact that it boasts the largest Australian Chamber of Commerce outside of Australia, and one of only two Australian International Schools in the world.

Left **Flowers for Chinese New Year** Centre **Bun Festival** Right **Dragon Dance, Tin Hau**

🔟 Festivals and Events

Fireworks, Chinese New Year

1 Chinese New Year
Hong Kong's most celebrated festival is a riot of neon and noise. Skyscrapers on both sides of the harbour are lit up to varying degrees depending on the vicissitudes of the economy, fireworks explode over the harbour, shops shut down and doormen suddenly turn nice, hoping for a handout of *lai see* (lucky money). 🚬 *Three days from the first day of the first moon, usually late Jan or early Feb*

2 Spring Lantern (Yuen Siu) Festival
Also known as Chinese Valentine's Day, this festival marks the end of the traditional Lunar New Year celebrations. Canoodling couples take to the parks under the gentle glow of lanterns and peeping Tom arrests surge. 🚬 *The 15th day of the lunar calendar (end Feb)*

3 Tin Hau Festival
This is the big one if you make your living from the sea. Fishermen make floral paper

Tin Hau Festival

offerings to Tin Hau, the goddess of the sea, hoping for fine weather and full nets. (Her views on overfishing and dragnetting aren't clear.) Try the temples at Stanley, Joss House Bay or Tin Hau Temple Road. 🚬 *The 23rd day of the 3rd moon (Apr)*

4 Cheung Chau Bun Festival
Talk about a bunfight. Young men used to scale 8-m (26-ft) towers covered in buns until in the 1970s they started falling off and the practice was banned. They still erect the odd bun edifice. 🚬 *The 6th day of 4th moon (May), Cheung Chau • Map C6*

5 Ching Ming
Also known as the grave-sweeping festival, *ching ming* literally means "clear and bright". Chinese families visit the graves of their ancestors to burn "Hell money", which resembles Monopoly money. 🚬 *First week of Apr*

6 Dragon Boat (Tuen Ng) Festival
Drums thunder and paddles churn the less-than-pristine waters of Hong Kong as garish craft vie for top honours. The festival commemorates Qu Yuan, a 3rd-century poet-statesman who drowned himself to protest against corrupt rulers. 🚬 *The 5th day of the 5th moon (early June), various venues*

Dragon boats

7 Hungry Ghost (Yue Laan) Festival

From the 14th day of the seventh moon, Chinese believe the gates of hell are thrown open and the undead run riot on earth for a month. Lots more "Hell money" goes up in smoke, as do various hillsides. Not a good time for hiking. ✪ *Roughly Jul, various locations*

8 Mid-Autumn Festival

One of the most picturesque of Hong Kong's festivals. Families brave the most appalling traffic jams to venture out into the country parks to burn candles and feast on yolk-centred moon-cakes. Unfortunately, the intricate paper lanterns have increasingly been supplanted by glowing, blow-up Hello Kitty, Doraemon and Pokémon dolls. ✪ *The 15th night of the 8th moon (Aug); try Victoria Park*

9 Chung Yeung Festival

Put on your hiking boots. This festival commemorates a Han Dynasty scholar who took his family up a hill and came back to find the rest of his village murdered. ✪ *The 9th evening of the 9th moon (usually mid- to late Oct); visit any hilltop*

10 Christmas Day

Not a traditional Chinese festival, of course, but Hong Kongers have wholeheartedly embraced the more commercial aspects of Christmas. ✪ *25th Dec*

Top 10 Sporting Events

1 Rugby 10s
Beer-swilling mayhem and fast and furious rugby. ✪ *HK Rugby Football Union • 2504 8311 • www.hkrugby.com • Mar*

2 Rugby Sevens
More of the above. ✪ *Week in Mar following the 10s*

3 Cricket Sixes
Action around the stumps. ✪ *Kowloon Cricket Club 2367 4141 • Nov*

4 International Dragon Boat Races
Festive boats compete on the Shing Mun River. ✪ *Sha Tin • mid-Jun*

5 International Races
Pounding equine competition. ✪ *Sha Tin Racecourse • HK Jockey Club 2966 8565 • Dec*

6 Carlsberg Cup
Soccer action. ✪ *Hong Kong Football Association 2712 9122 • Late Jan*

7 Standard Chartered Hong Kong Marathon
The gruelling race starts at the Cultural Centre, Tsim Sha Tsui. ✪ *2577 0800 • Early Feb*

8 Macau Grand Prix
Formula 3 action on the former Portuguese enclave. ✪ *796 2268 (Macau); 2838 8680 (Hong Kong) • 3rd weekend Nov*

9 Trailwalker
A gruelling 60-mile (100-km) walk over MacLehose Trail, in aid of the charity Oxfam. ✪ *Oxfam 2520 2525 • Nov*

10 Omega Hong Kong Open
Asia's top golfing stars on show. ✪ *Asian PGA 2330 8227 • Late Nov*

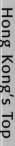

Left **Temple Street** Centre left **Western Market** Centre right **Bird Market** Right **Goldfish Market**

🔟 Markets

1 Temple Street
Comes alive at night. Hundreds of stalls are jam-packed by 9pm, offering pirated goods and all manner of, well, junk. It used to be known as Men's Street, and many stalls still stock less-than-fashionable attire. Venture past the market and you'll stumble onto a lamplit coterie of fortune-tellers and possibly a Chinese Opera recital. *(See pp18–19.)*

2 Western Market
The Western Market (in the northwest of Hong Kong Island) is situated in a gorgeous old Edwardian building, but the pickings are slim. Best bet is the excellent selection of antique and second-hand watches on the ground floor. Also a good range of fabric shops, although bargains are scarce. In a former life it housed a meat and vegetable market. ⊗ *323 Des Voeux Rd Central, Sheung Wan • Map J4 • 10am–7pm*

3 Ladies Market
No designer labels – unless they're fake. What you'll find here is inexpensive women's clothing from lingerie to shoes. There's a decent selection of jeans, cheap food and knick-knacks galore. *(See p90.)*

4 Jardine's Bazaar and Jardine's Crescent
An open-air market area in the heart of Causeway Bay, one of Hong Kong's busiest shopping districts. All sorts of goodies here, from run-of-the-mill fashion shops to traditional barbers and Chinese medicine sellers. Sample a glass of fresh soy bean milk. ⊗ *Jardine's Bazaar, Causeway Bay, Hong Kong Island • Map Q6 • 11am–8pm*

5 Cat Street
No, there are no more cats here than anywhere else in Hong Kong. Cat Street refers instead to the Chinese slang for odds and ends. It and nearby

Left **Antique Buddha image, Cat Street** Right **Mao posters, Cat Street**

Busy Gage Street Market

Hollywood Road are chock full of antique and curio shops. This is the place for silk carpets, elegant Chinese furniture, Ming dynasty ceramic horsemen and Maoist kitsch. ◎ Map J5

6 Jade Market
As you might suppose, jade sellers abound – more than 450 of them at last count. Don't attempt to buy the top-grade stuff unless you're an expert and know what you are doing. But there are plenty of cheaper pieces to be found (see p90).

7 Stanley Market
Full of tourists of the badge-sporting, flag-following variety. If you're not claustrophobic, join the hordes thronging the narrow lanes to gorge on tacky rubbish. (See also p16.) ◎ Stanley Main Rd, Hong Kong Island • Map F6 • 10am–6pm

8 Bird Market
More than 70 stalls showcasing all manner of songbirds and (mostly legal) exotica, bounded by elegant courtyards, full of old men with white singlets rolled up to bare their bellies (one of Hong Kong's odder fashion statements). A flower market is also nearby (see p89). ◎ Yuen Po Street, Mong Kok • 7am–8pm

9 Goldfish Market
Popular spot for locals, as a fishtank in the right spot is thought to ward off bad luck. Hook a bargain on underwater furniture with an oriental flavour. ◎ Tung Choi St, Mong Kok • 10am–6pm

10 Gage Street
This one is worth a peek if you happen to be in Central but hardly worth a special visit. Lots of blood and guts, especially for early birds. Trucks disgorge fresh pink pig carcasses as squawking chickens ponder their final hours. ◎ Map K5

Left **Mid-Level escalator** Centre **Rickshaw** Right **Open-top bus**

🔟 Transports of Delight

1 The Escalator
The series of escalators in the steep Mid-Levels district of northwest Hong Kong Island is designed for commuters, but most appreciated by sightseers who can rest their legs and enjoy the fascinating sights *(opposite)*. Take a stately (and free) ascent past busy street scenes, traditional shops and apartment windows. *(See p59.)*

2 Trams
Hong Kong's trams date back to 1904, making this one of the oldest continuously used tram systems in existence. They are still one of the best ways of exploring the Hong Kong Island shoreline. Trainspotter's trivia: it's also the only double-decker tram system in the whole world.

Old-fashioned tram

3 The Peak Tram
Since 1888, this funicular railway has made the jaw-dropping ascent of Victoria Peak and remains a must for visitors. Under the unwritten rules of colonial times, certain seats were reserved for high officials; now, seating is an amiable free-for-all. *(See p9.)*

4 Airport Express Link
Should your attention span wane on the fleeting 22-minute ride from the airport to Central, the AEL offers personal TVs in the back of every seat. Bright, shiny and a joy to use.

5 MTR
Hong Kong's underground railway is a world leader, handling three million people a day with rapid and robotic efficiency. Signs are in both English and Chinese, delays are almost unheard of, and with fares starting from the price of a cup of coffee, a trip around the city is surprisingly affordable, too.

6 Ferries
The fabulous Star Ferry *(see pp14–15)* connects Hong Kong Island to Kowloon. Pay half the price of a cup of coffee for a first-class view of one of the world's most remarkable harbours and skylines. Other ferries connect Hong Kong to the outlying islands and parts of the New Territories *(see p138).*

For more on getting around Hong Kong See p138

Rickshaws

7 There are just seven rickshaws left in all Hong Kong, their elderly drivers earning a living by charging tourists for photos. Don't ask for a ride, unless you want richly-deserved abuse from passers-by: these old guys can't make their way halfway down the road without collapsing in an exhausted heap.

Taxis

8 Hong Kong cabbies are as psychotic as big city cabbies everywhere. Their rudeness is legendary, but you probably would be too if you had to deal with Hong Kong traffic all day, every day. Fortunately, tighter policing means that overcharging is now a rare occurrence.

Limousines

9 On a per capita basis, Hong Kong probably has more Mercedes and Rolls Royces than anywhere else in the world. Some 50 of the latter are owned by the Peninsula Hotel alone – the largest Rolls Royce fleet in the world.

Buses

10 Hong Kong's double-decker buses are a British legacy, though these mostly come air-conditioned and (in a universally loathed development) with onboard TVs blaring ceaseless advertising. The low cost of using them may help you overcome this irritant.

Star ferries

Top 10 Sights from the Escalator

1 Escalator Itself
The world's longest covered escalator system is a sight unto itself.

2 Commuters
Some 211,000 people ride the system daily, bypassing the Mid-Levels' notorious traffic snarls.

3 Central Market
The escalator begins opposite this agreeably raucous fruit and vegetable market.

4 BoHo
("Below Hollywood Road") The start of the journey takes you through the heart of this hip quarter.

5 SoHo
("South of Hollywood Road"). Alight at the first stop and walk a block uphill for trendy bars and eateries (see p60).

6 Hollywood Road
Home to antique shops, galleries, nightclubs, bars and the historic Man Mo Temple (see p61).

7 Galleries
Several en route, many specializing in the bright new wave of Chinese art.

8 Rednaxela Terrace
So named because a 19th-century signwriter wrote "Alexander" from right to left, in the Chinese manner. Uncorrected to this day.

9 Jamia Masjid Mosque
Also known as the Shelly Street Mosque, built in 1915. One of three mosques catering to 70,000 Muslims.

10 Conduit Road
Where SoHo peters out, and the Mid-Levels begins amid forests of upscale apartment blocks.

Left **Bank of China, Cheung Kong Centre and HSBC** Right **Convention Centre**

TOP 10 Modern Buildings

HSBC interior

1 HSBC Building
Sir Norman Foster's striking, Bladerunner-esque edifice cost a whopping HK$5.2bn, making it the world's priciest pile when it opened in 1985. The headquarters of the Hong Kong and Shanghai Banking Corporation are reputed to have some of the best feng shui around – the building sits on a rare confluence of five "dragon lines" and enjoys unimpeded harbour views. The soaring atrium feels like a cathedral, which might explain why on Sundays the ground level is taken over by chattering Filipina maids. ◎ *1 Queen's Rd, Central • Map L5*

Bank of China

2 Bank of China
This one is also famous in feng shui circles, but more for dishing it out than possessing it – the glass-skinned tower shoot bad vibes at the old Governmen House and other colonial entities. Its knife-like edges wer the inspiration of American-Chinese master architect I. M. Pei. The 70-storey, 368-m (1,207 ft) stack of prisms opened in 1990. Its viewing platform is the natural place to go for a sweeping city perspective. ◎ *1 Garden R Central • Map L6 • 43/F viewing platforr 9am–6pm Mon–Fri, 9am–1pm Sat*

3 Tsing Ma Bridge
The suspension bridge stre tches from Tsing Yi Island to Lan tau, a mile and a half (2.2 km) long A striking sight, especially wher lit up at night, the bridge carries the road and rail links to Chek Lap Kok airport. It opened in Ma 1997, having taken five years to build at a cost of HK$7.14 bn.
Take the MTR to Tsin Yi or catch an airport bus to view it – it can't be seen from th Airport Railway. There's also a viewing platform at Ting Kau *(see p116)*. ◎ *Map D4*

4 Two IFC Tower
Completed in 2003, the streamline Two International Finance Centre Tower soars high above Vic-

ria Harbour. At 420 m (1,378 ft),
is Hong Kong's tallest building
nd the third tallest in the world.
he shopping mall at its base is
ne of the biggest on the island.
Exchange Square, Central • Map L5

5 Hong Kong International Airport
r Norman Foster strikes again.
anding isn't quite the thrill ride
was at the old airport, but the
ew passenger terminal, which
pened in July 1998, is impressive.
ne airport is constructed on a
pecially flattened island – Chek
ap Kok. ◉ *Map B4*

6 Lippo Towers
These knobbly megaliths
ok like they have koalas cling-
g to the sides – a reflection of
ne original antipodean owner,
ilbird Alan Bond. ◉ *89 Queensway,
dmiralty • Map L–M6*

7 The Centre
The one with the pretty col-
urs that keep changing all night
 fantastic, unless you live next
oor. One of tycoon Li Ka-shing's
iumphs. ◉ *Queen's Rd • Map K5*

8 Cheung Kong Centre
Big, boxy and glassy,
nother one of Li's babies, on
ne site of the old Hilton. He

Lippo Towers

lives on the top of this one. Note
how it's built perfectly parallel to
the adjoining Bank of China for
optimal feng shui. ◉ *Map L6*

9 Central Plaza
Confusingly, this is in Wan
Chai, not Central. At 78 storeys,
it is two less than The Centre,
but at 374 m (1,227 ft), it's taller.
It's also the world's tallest
reinforced concrete building. ◉ *18
Harbour Rd, Wan Chai • Map N5 • 46/F
viewing platform 9am–5pm Mon–Fri*

10 HK Convention and Exhibition Centre
Site of the official Handover
ceremony in 1997, the Centre
sprawls over a huge area over
the harbour and was designed to
resemble a bird in flight. ◉ *1 Expo
Drive, Wan Chai • Map N5*

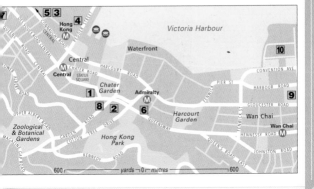

Left **Sai Kung peninsula** Centre **Birdlife, Mai Po Marshes** Right **Ma On Shan**

Areas of Natural Beauty

Cape D'Aguilar

It may be only 7 miles (11 km) directly south of Hong Kong's busy Central district, but Cape D'Aguilar feels like another world. The wild coastline has wave-lashed rock formations and a marine life so rich that researchers have discovered 20 species "new to science" in these waters. ◈ Map F6

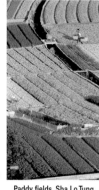

Paddy fields, Sha Lo Tung

Hoi Ha Wan

The long inlets and sheltered coves of this 260 hectare marine park in northern Sai Kung are made for snorkelling. Stony coral and reef fish galore. ◈ Map G2

Mai Po Marsh

Declared a Ramsar site (that is, a wetland of international importance) in 1995, Mai Po is one of China's most important bird sanctuaries, with hundreds of resident and migratory species recorded including many endangered ones. Other wildlife include otters, civet cats, bat and numerous amphibians. ◈ Map D2

Bride's Pool

The pool is a popular picnic spot. Weekends are best avoided, but visit midweek and, with luck, you will have the glorious, wooded course of rockpools and cascades all to yourself. ◈ Map F

Pat Sin Range

Hong Kong's countryside achieves a quiet grandeur among the empty valleys and sublime uplands of Pat Sin ("eight spirits"). Peaks range up to 639 m (2,095 ft), and the views are humbling. ◈ Map F2

Left **Bride's Pool** Centre **River valley, Pat Sin**

Sharp Peak and Ham Tin beach, Tai Long Wan

6 The Dragon's Back
This undulating ridge snakes down Hong Kong Island's south-east corner, with plunging slopes, poetic sea views and (past Pottinger's Gap) deep wooded valleys and beaches. ◈ Map F5

7 Jacob's Ladder
Take these steep steps up the rock from Three Fathom's Cove, and enter an expanse of remote uplands and boulder-strewn paths, leading, in the north, to Mount Hallowes. There are exquisite views of the Tolo Channel. ◈ Map G3

8 Sha Lo Tung
This hidden valley is probably the closest Hong Kong comes to stereotypical ideas of classical Chinese landscape, with its old paddy fields, deserted villages, flowing streams and ancient woods. Magical. ◈ Map F2

9 Ma On Shan
The plateaus and grassy slopes of the 702-m ((2,302-ft) high Ma On Shan ("Saddle Mountain") allow wide-screen views of mountainous country, without the insidious intrusion of city skyline in the distance. The effect is truly majestic. ◈ Map F3

10 Tai Long Wan
On the Sai Kung Peninsula, survive the knuckle-whitening ascent of Sharp Peak (all loose rocks and narrow paths), and the land plunges down to your well-earned reward: the sparkling waves and white sand of Hong Kong's finest beach, Tai Long Wan (see pp22–3).

For more areas of natural beauty **See p105**

45

Left **Cultural Centre promenade** Centre **View from the Peak** Right **Fortune tellers, Temple Street**

Walking Routes and Promenades

1 The Peak Circuit

Taking about an hour to complete at a gentle pace, this loop around Victoria Peak, formed by Harlech and Lugard Roads, offers jaw-dropping city panoramas to the north, boundless sea views to the south, and glimpses of millionaire homes among the greenery en route (see pp8–9).

2 Temple Street Night Market

Allow plenty of time, not for the distance (Temple Street is no more than half a mile end to end), but to explore the funky pageantry of hawker stalls, fortune tellers, medicine men and opera singers that set up here every night (see pp18–19).

3 The MacLehose Trail

The trail spans over 60 miles (100 km) across the New Territories, so only bona fide outdoor types will attempt the whole length. But certain sections are easily accessible (try the lovely part around the High Island Reservoir) for visitors who value the prospect of being back at the hotel bar by nightfall. ⊗ Info from HKTB (see p139) • Map G3

4 Central to Western via Hollywood Road

Central's futuristic office towers and concrete canyons give way to the low-rise charm of antique shops, galleries and bars the further west you go, ending up in Western's archetypal Chinese shopping streets and docksides. A must. (See also pp58–61.)

5 Cultural Centre Promenade

On weekends this short walkway from Kowloon Star Ferry around past the Inter-Continental is invaded by innumerable families and their rampaging children. At other times, though, it offers one of the most animated harbour views you will see anywhere (see pp82–3).

6 Nathan Road

A joyously tacky and tawdry strip, the Golden Mile, Hong Kong's own Broadway, runs up the Kowloon peninsula, passing hotels and tourist shops at the

Left **Quiet road at the Peak** Right **Temple Street Night Market**

Left Nathan Road at night Right Cheung Chau

upscale southern end, before downgrading into the sleazy karaoke lounges and low-rent storefronts of central Kowloon. Just don't buy any electronics along the way. (See p81.)

7 The Hong Kong Land Loop

Almost all of Central's prestige commercial towers are in the portfolio of one company, Hong Kong Land, which has thoughtfully connected its properties with aerial walkways. The buildings include Jardine House, Mandarin Oriental, Princes Building and the Landmark Centre. Do the circuit, if only for the ethereal experience of seeing downtown Hong Kong without touching the ground. ◈ Map L5

8 The Praya, Cheung Chau

This island *praya* (or waterfront road) is everything the main drag of a backwater fishing town should be: a rambling tableau of fresh catches, boats lying up, market stalls and skipping kids. Look out for the splendid hand-pulled

Surfer, Cheung Chau

water carts that are the island's only fire engines (see pp24–5).

9 The Central Green Trail

Just minutes from the banks, malls and offices of downtown, this signposted, hour-long trail from the tram terminus at Hong Kong Park opens up a lush hillside world of trees, ferns and rocks. A beautiful, shady surprise. ◈ Map L6

10 Victoria Park

One of the city's larger green sites, Victoria Park is best visited in the early morning, when tai chi devotees exercise. Throughout the day there are people-watching opportunities and restful walks, away from urban pressures (see pp68–9).

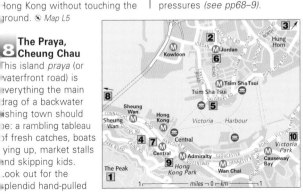

Left **Alibi** Right **Kam Tak Lam**

🍽️10 Restaurants

1 T'ang Court
The Langham Hotel completed its US$35 million upgrade in 2003, and the food at T'ang Court continues to astonish. Peerless creativity and an insistence on *wok chi* (wok cooking at the highest achievable temperature) are the keys to T'ang Court's greatness. ◈ *1/F, Langham Hotel, 8 Peking Road, Kowloon • Map N4 • 2375 1133 ext. 2250 • $$$$*

2 The Verandah
From its epic Sunday brunches, through to the speechless aplomb of its candlelit dinners, this sleek patrician of the Southside has a stately lead over the competition. The details are sheer class (when did you last have caesar salad made, as it should be, at your tableside?) and the ambience utterly surfeited with the "wow" factor *(see p77)*.

3 Gaddi's
Royalty, Hollywood stars and heads of state have dined here by the worshipful score, for in terms of French cuisine east of Suez, Gaddi's is unquestionably the holy grail. Expect the big-budget works: from the aristocratic menu to stratospheric service levels. If you like it *haute*, you've found your heaven *(see p87)*.

4 Nicholini's
You might not foresee yourself travelling to Hong Kong in order to eat Italian, but you might for Nicholini's. Awarded the Insegna del Romano for being the best Italian restaurant outside of Italy, Nicholini's sits comfortably at the apex of Northern Italian cooking, each dish an essay in freshness and charm ◈ *8/F, Conrad International, Pacific Place, Admiralty • Map N4 • 2521 3838 • $$$$*

5 Alibi
If there has been one Hong Kong restaurateur consistently and laudably pushing the style envelope over the last decade, it has been Nichole Garnaut. But with Alibi, her latest venture, she succeeds with understatement,

Left **The Verandah** Right **One Harbour Road**

Jimmy's Kitchen

and the creative take on French cuisine has both depth and confidence. The crowd is beautiful, the food more so *(see p65)*.

6 M at the Fringe

The totality of M's undeniable quirks – the mismatching cutlery, eccentric menu, the arty location (above the galleries of the Fringe Club) – come together in a riotously groovy whole. The food is Mediterranean and Middle Eastern influenced, although simply stating this does no justice to its free form improvisation of flavours. Superior stuff *(see p65)*.

Fringe Club

7 One Harbour Road

Cantonese cuisine is the most artful of Chinese provincial varieties, and One Harbour Road is among the most artful of Cantonese restaurants. Be prepared then for a dining experience of unusual refinement, set off by the Grand Hyatt's art deco fantasies. The restaurant endlessly wins deserved praise. ◆ *8/F, Grand Hyatt, 1 Harbour Road, Wan Chai • Map N4 • 2588 1234 • $$$$*

8 The Mandarin Grill

So moneyed, clubbish and upholstered, you could be sitting in St James's in London.

Except for the food: no London grill room could ever approximate the exemplary filets and sirloins turned out here. We are talking consummate mastery of skillet and skewer. No wonder the suits linger for hours over brandy and cigars *(see p65)*.

9 Kung Tak Lam

Vegetarians unable to face another helping of the slop and swill that passes for much animal-free cuisine will praise the creator for Kung Tak Lam. This light and airy Shanghainese does things with mere vegetables that could not be done, could not even be imagined, by most vegetarian restaurants elsewhere. ◆ *31 Yee Wo St, Causeway Bay • Map N4 • 2890 3127 • $$*

10 Jimmy's Kitchen

If you have longed for the day when you would stumble on a restaurant locked in a parallel 1970s universe – where the menu offers, without irony, such wide-collared classics as chicken Kiev and baked Alaska – then rejoice. For this is that day; Jimmy's is that restaurant. Don't pass up on a chance like this *(see p65)*.

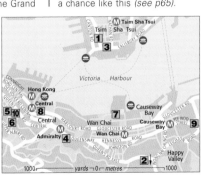

Left *Cha siu* Centre Fish drying, Cheung Chau Right Pak-choi

🔟 Hong Kong Dishes

1 Cha Siu
This is virtually Hong Kong's national dish. The name literally means "blacken and burn", but it's neither. The tender fillets of pork are roasted and glazed in honey and spices, and hung in the windows of specialist roast meat shops. *Cha siu* is classically served thinly sliced, with steamed rice and strips of vegetables.

2 Moon Cake
Made of moist pastry and various fillings, including lotus, taro, adzuki bean, whole egg yolk and occasionally coconut, the delicacy also has a quirky history: revolutionaries in imperial China used to smuggle messages to each other hidden in a moon cake's dense filling.

3 Steamed Whole Fish
In Hong Kong, fish is almost always dressed very simply, using only peanut oil, soya sauce, coriander and chives. To maximize

Steamed whole fish

freshness, restaurants keep live fish in tanks, killing and preparing them to order.

4 Hainan Chicken
Comprising chunks of steamed chicken, served slightly warm or cold, and dipped in an aromatic oil made with spring onions and ginger, this dish has become everyday comfort food. It is traditionally accompanied by a rich chicken broth, a few vegetables and rice steamed in chicken stock for flavour.

5 Brisket of Beef
Requiring up to eight hours of slow cooking, preparation of this Hong Kong classic is an art. Households and restaurants guard their individual recipes, but all involve the classic five Chinese spices, rock sugar and tangerine peel. It's served in an earthenware pot as a main course, or as a topping for rice or noodles. Given its richness, it is particularly enjoyed in winter.

6 Water Spinach
The leafy, hollow-stemmed vegetable can be prepared with various seasonings, from the quotidian oyster sauce to garlic and shrimp paste. At its best when stir-fried with potent chillies and semi-fermented tofu.

Dried meats

Wonton soup

7 Wontons
Done properly, this marvellous prawn and pork ravioli is poached in a stock made from shrimp roe, aniseed and other spices, and served with fresh egg noodles and soup.

8 Fish Balls
A daily food for many Hong Kongers, either on skewers as snacks or served with noodles in broth to make a meal. Traditional restaurants eschew machine production methods, and still shape these balls of minced fish, white pepper and other spices by hand, before poaching them in seafood or chicken stock.

9 Salt and Pepper Crusted Squid
You may have encountered the disastrous and greasy travesty of fried squid served up in Western Chinatowns. Banish that unpleasant memory from your mind, and prepare to discover the gloriously crisp original. Fresh squid is scored, lightly battered and flash fried with lots of salt, white pepper, chilli and garlic. The result is an addictive combination of tangy textures.

10 Lai Wong Bau
Chinese bread is shaped into buns, not loaves, and steamed rather than baked – giving it a beautifully soft and fluffy quality (no gritty whole grains here). There are many varieties of sweet bun, but *lai wong bau* is the reigning favourite, the kind of treat that children will clamour for. These buns are filled with milk, eggs, coconut and sugar. Try them piping hot on a cold winter morning.

Top 10 Dim Sum (Dumplings)

1 Ha Gow
Prawns wrapped in rice flour casing – like a very plump ravioli.

2 Siu Mai
Minced pork and shrimp parcels, topped with a dab of crab roe.

3 Seen Juk Guen
Soy pastry, crisp fried with a vegetable filling. A savvy alternative to the common spring roll.

4 Gai Jaht
Chicken and ham wrapped in soya bean sheets, served in rich sauce.

5 Lohr Bahk Goh
Mashed turnip, pan-fried with chives, dried shrimp and Chinese salami.

6 Cheung Fun
Rolls of rice pastry, filled with shrimp, pork or beef, and smothered in sweet soy.

7 Chiu Chow Fun Gohr
Soft, pasty-style dumplings filled with chopped nuts, minced pork and pickled vegetables.

8 Chin Yeung Laht Jiu
Green pepper stuffed with minced fish and prawns and served in black bean sauce.

9 Ji Ma Wu
Decadent, treacle-like dessert made from sugar and mashed sesame. It is served warm from the trolley.

10 Ma Lai Goh
Wonderfully light, steamed sponge cake, made with eggs and walnuts.

Left **The Jazz Club** Right **Visage Free**

TOP 10 Nightclubs

1 Felix

The shining pinnacle of Hong Kong bars is set in Kowloon's famous Peninsula Hotel. Philippe Starcke designed Felix, and the result is coolness incarnate. Let the experience envelope you, beginning with the dedicated elevators and their light effects, to the untrammelled delights of Felix's restrooms. The harbour views are an added bonus. If you plan to visit just one bar in Hong Kong, make this the one (see p87).

2 Foreign Correspondents Club

Any club that has brass plaques screwed to the bar top, commemorating members who died drinking on that spot, deserves to be a legend. Open only to members and their guests.
§ 2 Lower Albert Rd, Central • Map K6 • 2521 1511

3 Club 64

One of Hong Kong's most genuinely integrated scenes can be found at this Lan Kwai Fong institution. The sixth month, fourth day numbers of the name refer to the 1989 Tiannanmen Square massacre. On a given night, Chinese DJs will be sat next to expatriate web editors and Nigerian bass guitarists. Club 64 has no spit or polish whatsoever, but the beer is cheap, and everyone's in the mood to talk (see p64).

Club 64

4 Kee

A discreet keypad and unmarked doorway on Wellington Street is the entrance to this spanking new and seriously happening club. Everyone worth knowing in Hong Kong is on its members' list, but this means that it can be hard to gain access. Inspired by the Enlightenment concept of literary and discursive salons, Kee can sometimes be too arty by half, but it's always worth an invitation. Assuming you're lucky enough to score one. § 6/F, 32 Wellington St, Central • Map K5 • 2186 1861

5 Antidote

With its white modular furnishings and trippy lighting, the décor is fit for a soirée of subscribers to top international design magazine Wallpaper. Some of Hong Kong's best DJs and sound systems (notably Digital Cutup Lounge) perform in this intimate room, to cosy audiences of Hong Kong's air-kissing fab young things (see p64).

6 Bottoms Up

Fulfill your sad James Bond fantasies in the padded, crepuscular interior of this 1970s topless bar, which was used as a location in The Man with the Golden Gun. It had more character under its legendary

Left **Antidote** Right **Central district at night**

original owner and ex-Windmill Girl, Pat Sephton. Don't despair: for kitsch factor alone, Bottoms Up will always be a worthy pit stop *(see p86).*

7 The Jazz Club

At ordinary times, this tiny and utterly unremarkable bar and performance space would hardly be worth mentioning. But when a maestro is in town, the Jazz Club is the scene of legendary, impromptu jams. Believe it or not, even the likes of Wynton Marsalis and Miles Davis have played here, right in the faces of the 100 or so people lucky enough to have been there at the time. ⦾ *2/F, 34 D'Aguilar St, Lan Kwai Fong • Map K5 • 2845 8477*

8 Visage Free

A slacker alternative to the unremitting trendiness of SoHo and BoHo, Visage Free is the kind of bar that can disregard commercial imperatives to mount monthly poetry readings. The crowd is loyal and diverse. ⦾ *Amber Lodge, 23 Hollywood Rd, BoHo • Map J5 • 2546 9780*

9 Feather Boa

Away from the rowdy main strip of Staunton Street bars sits this unmarked gem, with its inconspicuous entrance, fin-de-siècle gold drapes and sofas. The crowd is young, arts and media-slanted, and cliquey. One of SoHo's better kept secrets: would it could stay that way *(see p64).*

10 Dance Parties

Hong Kong is a prime Asian stop on the international DJ circuit (everyone from Fat Boy Slim to Paul Oakenfold and Carl Cox have hit the decks here), and the city has nurtured more than enough turntable talent of its own. Hong Kong's dance parties, particularly at the cavernous HITEC venue, are well-organized affairs. Check the local media for details. ⦾ *Various venues*

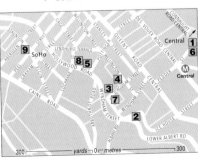

Left **Dolphin watching** Centre **Rollercoaster, Ocean Park** Right **Child, Kowloon Park**

TOP 10 Places for Children

1 Ocean Park
It's not quite Disneyland, but most kids will get a kick out of the dolphin and sea lion shows and the spectacular chairlift. It's a bit weak on rides, although this has been remedied somewhat in recent years with the advent of Adventure Land, featuring the Mine Train rollercoaster and Raging River ride. Threaten misbehaving brats with a dose of Middle Kingdom, the history and culture section. *(See p73.)*

Ocean Park

2 Science Museum
There is lots of hands-on stuff here, providing a fun and educational introduction to many facets of science. Any child with a healthy dose of curiosity will spend hours pushing buttons, pulling levers and marvelling at gadgets. *(See p82.)*

3 Zoological and Botanical Gardens
Founded in 1864, a modicum of Victorian gentility survives here in the wrought-iron bandstand and shrub-lined paths. Not, however, in the monkey house, where the world's largest collection of red-cheeked gibbons shriek and swing and copulate. Be prepared for some judicious covering of young eyes. Also jaguars, leopards, kangaroos and 280 species of birds. ✆ *Upper Albert Rd, Central • Map K6 • 6am–7pm daily • Free*

4 Dolphin Watching
Be quick, because the sorry state of Hong Kong waters is fast killing off the rare Chinese white dolphins, which, by the way, are really pale pink. ✆ *Hong Kong Dolphinwatch 1528A Star House, Tsim Sha Tsui • Map B4 (dolphins) • 2984 1414 • Bus pick-up 8:20am at Mandarin Oriental in Central and 8:50am at Kowloon Hotel TST • Wed, Fri, Sun • Adm*

5 Ripley's Believe It Or Not
The usual array of freaks and geeks. But the tram ride up the Peak is always a thrill, and you can also check out the Peak Explorer, a multimedia motion

Left **Jaguar, Zoological Gardens** Right **Peak tram**

Left **Ripley's Believe It or Not** Right **Old-fashioned tram**

simulator ride through space, and Madame Tussaud's waxworks museum. ◈ Level 3, Peak Tower, 128 Peak Road • 2849 7654 • Map E5 • 10am–10pm daily • Adm

6 Lions Nature Education Centre

The Lions Nature Education Centre is actually much more fun than it sounds. There are fruit orchards, an arboretum, rock gardens and, best of all, an insectarium. Big brothers will find plenty of interesting creepy-crawlies with which to scare little sisters. ◈ Tsiu Hang, Sai Kung, New Territories • Map G3 • 2792 2234 • 9:30am–5pm. Closed Tue • Free

7 Ice Skating

The most accessible rink is at Taikooshing, a big shopping centre and housing estate on the eastern part of Hong Kong Island. Once in, you can skate for as long as you like on weekdays. The skating school takes over on weekends.
◈ Taikooshing • Map F5 • Adm

8 Tram Tour

Rock, rattle and roll along the front of Hong Kong Island, or take a detour around Happy Valley. Hong Kong's trams may be crowded, slow and noisy, but they are terrific for sightseeing. (See p138.)

9 Kowloon Park

The green lungs of Tsim Sha Tsui have a huge indoor-outdoor swimming pool and lots of gardens to wander about. There's also an aviary. (See p83.)

10 Snoopy World

Good grief! Hang out with the famous beagle and his hapless master Charlie Brown in this colourful tribute to the late Charles Schulz's much-loved comic strip. Two-metre (6-ft) high mechanical characters and 60 other Peanuts figures inhabit the playground. ◈ L3 Podium, New Town Plaza, Sha Tin, New Territories • Map E3 • 2601 9178 • 10am–10pm • Free

HONG KONG'S TOP 10

Left **Red lory, Hong Kong Park** Centre **One of the escalators** Right **Central district and harbour**

Hong Kong Island – Northwest

FROM THE CORPORATE VANITIES of Central district's glass towers, through the vodka bars and galleries of SoHo, and spilling down flagstone lanes to the raucous shophouses and old docksides of Western, the Island's northwest potently concentrates all of Hong Kong's surreal contradictions. In the concrete gullies between futuristic banks and statement office blocks you'll find traditional street markets, temples and herbalists, all carrying on like some Hollywood dream of old Chinatown. These are some of the most mercantile streets in human history. A shot of snake bile wine, or a fierce macchiato? In this part of the city, you can have it all.

🔟 Sights in the Northwest

1. Hong Kong Park
2. Exchange Square and Two International Finance Centre Tower
3. Former Government House
4. The Escalator
5. SoHo
6. Sheung Wan and Western
7. Lan Kwai Fong
8. The Waterfront
9. Man Mo Temple
10. Hollywood Road

Man Mo Temple

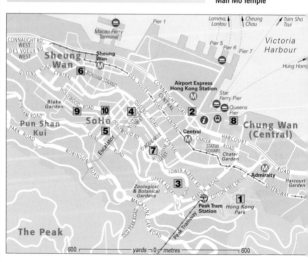

Aviary, Hong Kong Park

1 Hong Kong Park

When you're tired of Central's relentless bustle, Hong Kong Park's open spaces and mature trees make an excellent escape, particularly its strikingly elegant (and free) walk-through aviary. The flowing streams and lush plant life of this improbable mini-rainforest are a peaceful and shaded home to scores of exotic bird species. The park also has lakes, a large conservatory, a viewing tower and the free Museum of Teaware, which is located inside Flagstaff House. ◈ *Map L6*

2 Exchange Square and Two IFC Tower

As the name suggests, Exchange Square houses Hong Kong's red-carpeted financial engine room, although the stock exchange is not open to visitors. However, the peaceful square outside it, dominated by a large fountain, is a great place to eat or drink outside. Near the fountain are sculptures by Henry Moore and Dame Elizabeth Frink. The square's newest building, Two IFC Tower *(see pp42–3)*, is a striking addition to the island's already impressive skyline. ◈ *Map L5*

3 Former Government House

This grand old building served as the British governor's residence from 1855 until 1997, when the last governor, Chris Patten, handed Hong Kong back to China. Patten's successor, Tung Chee Hwa, cited bad feng shui created by the needle-like Bank of China building *(see p42)* as one reason not to move in, opting to remain in his house on the Peak. Back in the 1940s, the occupying Japanese added the Shinto-style towers to the Georgian structure, which at one time enjoyed harbour views. The building is used for official functions, only opening occasionally to the public – contact HKTB *(see p139)* for details. ◈ *Map L6*

4 The Escalator

A wonderful feature of Hong Kong is its 792-m (2,598-ft) long string of escalators, which links all the roads between Queen's Road and Conduit Street. It's the best way for pedestrians to get around the steep districts of Central, the Mid-Levels and SoHo. The Escalator runs uphill until midnight, except during the morning rush hour, when it runs downhill. ◈ *Map K5*

Frink sculpture, Exchange Square

For the top 10 sights from the Mid-Levels Escalator **See p41**

Left **Restaurant, SoHo** Right **Antiques, Hollywood Road**

5 SoHo

In the last few years SoHo (so-called for being the area south of Hollywood Road) has been transformed from a sleepy district of traditional Chinese shops into a thriving area for hip bars, cafés and restaurants. Elgin, Shelley and Staunton streets are excellent places to find a drink or bite to eat. ◎ *Map K5*

6 Sheung Wan and Western

The older, more traditional Chinese areas of town, just west of Central's sleek corporate headquarters and the smart shops, are worth exploring by foot. The reward is a fascinating array of shops, mostly wholesalers, selling dried seafood (the pervading smell here), ginseng, edible swallows' nests, snakes, arcane herbal ingredients and paper offerings for the dead. Try the streets around Bonham Strand. ◎ *Map J4*

7 Lan Kwai Fong

Not much to look at during the day, Lan Kwai Fong (or Orchid Square) only really starts to buzz at night when office workers, including plenty of city suits, come here to unwind at its many bars, clubs and restaurants. The street is packed with revellers on Fridays. The partying spills

across to tiny Wing Wah Lane just across D'Aguilar Street with bars and good-value Thai, Malay and Indian restaurants. ◎ *Map K5*

8 The Waterfront

Turn right out of the Central Star Ferry for some (admittedly meagre and poorly exploited) open waterside space and benche with good views across to

Man Mo Temple

For Central's Statue Square **See pp10–11**

entral district

owloon. Behind are the 1,700
orthole-style windows of Jardine
ouse, for many years Asia's
allest building. To the east is the
iant upturned gin bottle shape
f the Prince of Wales HQ building,
ow one of the Chinese army's
ain Hong Kong barracks.
◎ *Map L–M5*

Man Mo Temple

9 The gloomy red and gold
terior of the Man Mo Temple,
ating back to the 1840s, is
ways thick with sandlewood
moke from the giant incense
pirals hanging overhead, which
ake a couple of weeks to burn
hrough. The temple is dedicated
two deities, Man (the god of
terature) and Mo (the god of
ar). Some of the scenes from
he film version of Richard
Mason's *The World of Suzy
Wong* were filmed here.
◎ *Western end, Hollywood Rd • Map J5*

Hollywood Road

10 This mecca for Chinese
ntiques and curios may no
onger offer the bargains it once
id but Hollywood Road's
astern end is still jammed with
hops selling ancient ceramics,
nammoth ivory carvings and
elicate snuff bottles. The stalls
nd shops on Upper Lascar Row
re a good hunting ground for
ntiques, trinkets, old coins,
itsch and curios. Haggling is
efinitely acceptable here.
◎ *Map J–K5*

A Day in Central

Morning

From Des Voeux Road take
the tram westwards from
Central and jump off
outside the handsome
colonial building housing
Western Market *(see
p38)*. Browse among the
ground floor trinkets,
select a pattern from the
many bolts of material on
the first floor and enjoy
excellent *dim sum* at the
upstairs restaurants.

The streets around nearby
Bonham Strand contain
dried seafood shops, Chi-
nese apothecaries, and
paper offering shops. Head
uphill to the atmospheric
Man Mo Temple, then
east past the antique shops
of **Hollywood Road**,
browsing as you go.

Break for lunch or a
drink in one of the many
restaurants and bars on
the streets to the south
(**SoHo**) or below
Hollywood Road in
Lan Kwai Fong.

Afternoon

Check out the fresh prod-
uce market stalls around
the **Escalator** *(see p59)*
and Graham Street before
hitting **Statue Square** *(see
pp10–11)*, the Island's
colonial heart.

Choose to visit the **upmarket malls** *(see p63)* or for
some peace and harbour
views head to Queen's
Pier, or for altitude and a
spectacular city perspec-
tive go up to the viewing
gallery high in the imposing,
needle-sleek **Bank of
China Building** *(see p42)*.

Quiet and shade are found
in the nearby **Hong Kong
Park** *(see p59)*.

Left **St John's Cathedral** Centre **Colonial Police Station** Right **Legco Building**

🔟 Colonial Relics

1 St John's Cathedral
It may resemble a parish church more than a cathedral but St John's, completed in 1850, is the oldest Anglican church in east Asia. ◎ *Map L6*

2 George VI Statue
In the Zoological and Botanical Gardens, the statue of King George VI was erected in 1941, to commemorate 100 years of British rule. ◎ *Map K6*

3 Colonial Street Names
Most colonial buildings have been sacrificed to new development, but the colonial legacy is preserved in many of the roads named after royals (Queen's Road), politicians (Peel Street), military officers (D'Aguilar, Pedder) and public servants (Bonham, Des Voeux). ◎ *Map K5–6*

4 Old Letter Box
A few traditional green, cast-iron post boxes bearing the British Royal Cipher remain. There is one at the northern end of Statue Square. ◎ *Map L5*

5 Former Military Hospital
Broken into separate units – some abandoned – the huge, grand old building between Bowen and Borrett roads used to serve as a Military Hospital. ◎ *Bowen Road • Map L6*

6 Hollywood Road Police Station
Bastions of colonial law and order, the Police Station and the old Victoria Prison still stand. ◎ *Map K5*

7 Flagstaff House
Built in the mid-1840s, Flagstaff House is one of the oldest colonial buildings on the island and today houses the free teaware museum. ◎ *Hong Kong Park • Map L6*

8 Duddell Street
While not spectacular, the gas lamps and old steps of Duddell Street date back to the 1870s. ◎ *Off Ice House St • Map K5*

9 Legco Building
The elegant Neo-Classical Legislative building, completed 1911, originally served as Hong Kong's Supreme Court and now functions as Hong Kong's would be parliament. ◎ *Map L5*

10 Mission Etrangeres
The handsome former French Mission building (built 1917) is Hong Kong's Court of Final Appeal, though that's not an apt name given that the court has referred some legal wrangle to Beijing. ◎ *Battery Path • Map L6*

ft **The Landmark Centre** Right **Lane Crawford**

10 Up-Market Malls and Boutiques

1 The Landmark Centre
It's impossible to miss this smart, modern mall, with its conspicuous consumables from the likes of Chanel, Dior, Zegna, Versace, Prada, Vuitton, Bulgari and Tiffany. ◈ *Pedder St • Map L5*

2 Seibu
Four floors of designer clothes, cosmetics, gifts, household items and food. ◈ *Pacific Place, 88 Queensway, Admiralty • Map M6*

3 Lane Crawford
Upmarket clothing, with concessions from most big Western designer brands, houseware, beauty products, glass and porcelain ranging from the exotic to the naff. ◈ *Pacific Place, 88 Queensway, Admiralty • Map M6*

4 The Prince's Building
Not as many top names as the next-door Landmark, but the bright, airy and less crowded Prince's Building is worth a visit if big-name clothes and accessory designers are your thing. ◈ *Statue Square & Des Voeux Rd • Map L5*

5 The Pedder Building
Not a top mall, but many shops offer clearance stocks of designer clothes at sharp mark-downs. Most specialise in women's fashions. ◈ *Pedder St • Map L5*

6 Gucci
This beautiful temple to the brand of Gucci is tended by elegant priestesses. It's merely a question of whether you can afford to worship here. ◈ *The Landmark Centre, G1 • Map L5*

7 Dragon Culture
Antiques shop with pottery from most dynasties, bamboo carvings and snuff bottles. ◈ *231 Hollywood Rd • Map K5*

8 Fetish Fashion
Fun and fetish goods go together in this smart store dedicated to cross-dressers and leather lovers. Look out for the family of leather teddy bears. ◈ *Merlin Bldg, 32 Cochrane St • Map K5*

9 Shanghai Tang
Local entrepreneur David Tang is the brains behind this smart twist on traditional Chinese clothes and ornaments. Jackets and kitsch Mao watches are staples. ◈ *The Pedder Bldg, Map L5*

10 David's Shirts
Off-the-shelf and hand-made shirts are the speciality of this Hong Kong institution. Allow a couple of days for the handmade shirts. ◈ *Mezzanine Flr, Mandarin Oriental, Queen's Rd • Map L5*

Left **Antidote** Centre **Club 64** Right **V13**

🔝10 Bars and Clubs

1 Antidote
All white interior and trippy lights in this cutting-edge, urban room down a back alley. ◎ *15–19 Hollywood Rd • Map K5 • 2526 6559*

2 Club 64
Named after the 4 July 1989 Tiananmen student massacres (sixth month, fourth day), Club 64 is a conspicuously left-leaning, agreeably funky, tile-floored dive for media types and anarchists. ◎ *12-14 Wing Wah Lane, Lan Kwai Fong • Map K5 • 2523 2801*

3 One Fifth
Unquestionably, this is Hong Kong's buzziest bar of the moment. Take in the fabulous crowd, soaring ceilings and big city vibe. Also written as 1/5. ◎ *9 Star St • Map K5 • 2520 2515*

4 V13
The epic selection of fla-voured vodkas will occupy the most jaded of drinkers. Raise a glass to the thirsty inmates of Victoria Prison opposite. ◎ *13 Old Bailey St • Map K5 • SoHo • 2802 1313*

5 Phi-b
Slick, attitudinal and with different DJs every night, it's hard to go wrong at Phi-b. On busy nights the party sprawls onto the street. ◎ *Lower Basement, 79 Wyndham St, SoHo • Map K5 • 2869 4469*

6 Feather Boa
A former antique shop, now a bar, but with much of its old stock left in situ. Like drinking in a camp relative's front room. ◎ *3 Staunton St, Soho • Map K5 • 2857 2586*

7 Club '97'
In its heyday, Madonna and Alain Delon drank at what was Post '97. It's quieter now, but that's no bad thing. ◎ *Upper grd flr 9–11 Lan Kwai Fong • Map K5 • 2810 9333*

8 The Chater Lounge
Whiskey tumblers you need two hands to lift, carpets thick enough to break ankles, and obscene cigars – the setting of Sinatran fantasy. For players only. ◎ *Ritz Carlton, 3 Connaught Rd, Central • Map L5 • 2877 6666*

9 Fringe Club
Hong Kong's alternative arts venue offers a respite from Lan Kwai Fong's rowdier beer halls. ◎ *2 Lower Albert Rd, Central • Map K6 • 2521 7485*

10 Rice Bar
Pioneering the trendification of this area, the Rice Bar is a nat-ural pit stop. It has a gay vibe, but straights are welcome. ◎ *22 Jervois St, Western • Map K5 • 2851 4800*

Price Categories

For a three-course meal for one with half a bottle of wine (or equivalent meal) and extra charges.	**$** under HK$100
	$$ HK$100–250
	$$$ HK$250–450
	$$$$ HK$450–600
	$$$$$ Over HK$600

Left **Blue** Right **Yung Kee**

🔟 Restaurants

1 Alibi
The guest list is fabulous (Naomi Campbell to Chow Yun-fat); the food masterful updates of French cuisine. ❧ *73 Wyndham St, SoHo • Map K5 • 2167 8989 • $$$*

2 The Mandarin Grill
Benchmark Cantonese cuisine of the highest order, vertiginous harbour views, and service levels that would shame an imperial court. ❧ *Mandarin Oriental, 5 Connaught Rd • Map L5 • 2522 0111 • $$$$*

3 M at the Fringe
One of Hong Kong's first true independents, M has matured into a genuinely loved institution without losing its original funkiness. ❧ *Level 1, 2 Lower Albert Rd • Map K6 • 2877 4000 • $$$$*

4 Blue
The glass frontage is integral: people come to be seen. But the high standard of modern Australian cuisine ensures it an enduring reputation. ❧ *43 Lyndhurst Terrace, SoHo • Map K5 • 2815 4005 • $$$*

5 IndoChine 1929
An evocation of old Hanoi: all wooden shutters and muted pastels. The menu is a deft presentation of Vietnam's regional cuisines. ❧ *2/F, California Tower, 30–32 D'Aguilar St • Map K5 • 2869 7399 • $$$$*

6 Ye Shanghai
The "chinois" décor includes booths, organza curtains and retro motifs, but the northern Chinese food is the genuine article. ❧ *One Pacific Place • Map M6 • 2918 9833 • $$$$*

7 Jimmy's Kitchen
A favourite for its naff décor (all dark wood and leather) and retro menu, Jimmy's has dished out comfort food for generations. ❧ *1–3 Wyndham St • Map K5 • 2526 5293 • $$$*

8 Yung Kee
From its headset-toting waitresses to its efficient poultry kitchen (serving up 300 birds a day), Yung Kee is a riotous operation. Try the roast goose. ❧ *32–40 Wellington St • Map K5 • 2522 1624 • $$$*

9 Joyce
More of a pageant than a restaurant, Joyce is a drop-in centre for Hong Kong's über wealthy. ❧ *The Atrium, One Exchange Square • Map L5 • 2810 0807 • $$$*

🔟 Kau Kee
Humble Kau Kee was once offered millions for its beef brisket noodle recipe. Taste and see why. This is a place of pilgrimage. ❧ *21 Gough St • Map J5 • 2850 5967 • No credit cards • $*

Left **Noonday gun** Right **Revolving restaurant, Hopewell Centre**

Hong Kong Island – Northeast

THE EAST OF THE ISLAND was the first to take up the population pressures of the nascent colonial capital of Victoria, and until the late 1970s had a low rent reputation. Some of that survives in the haggard pole-dancing clubs and tattoo parlours of Wan Chai, the quarter where Richard Mason wrote The World Of Suzie Wong, and where generations of sailors have nursed hangovers. But today, you're far more likely to run into Starbucks, serviced apartments and highly costed office space. The night races at Happy Valley are where you'll see Hong Kongers at their most fevered, while in Causeway Bay is the neon of restaurants and boutiques. Further out, there are worthy surprises among the unlovely warehouses and office blocks of Quarry Bay and Chai Wan – live jazz, microbreweries and dance clubs.

🔟 Sights in the Northeast

1 Central Plaza
2 Noonday Gun
3 Convention and Exhibition Centre
4 Lockhart Road
5 "Old" Wan Chai
6 Happy Valley Racecourse
7 Hopewell Centre
8 Victoria Park
9 Causeway Bay Typhoon Shelter
10 Tin Hau Temple

Neon, "Old" Wan Chai

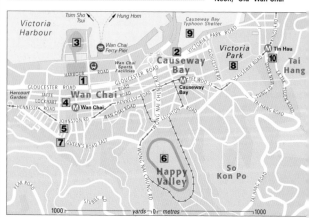

Central Plaza

3 Convention and Exhibition Centre

The building looks a bit like the Sydney Opera House might if its roof had just been swatted by a giant hammer. The designers, however, maintain that the flowing lines are meant to evoke a bird in flight. It's certainly a study in contrast with the upthrust towers scratching the sky all around. There was a race against time to finish stage two of the $5 billion complex in time for the 1997 Handover ceremony. Britain's loss and China's gain is commemorated with a big black obelisk. The venue also hosts occasional raves and pop concerts. ✈ *1 Harbour Rd, Wan Chai • Map N5 • 2582 8888*

4 Lockhart Road

Made famous in Richard Mason's novel *The World of Suzy Wong*, Wan Chai's sinful strip is these days an odd blend of girlie bars with doddery *Mamasans* who saw action during the Vietnam War and will rob you blind as soon as look at you; down-at-heel discos; mock-British pubs; and super-trendy bars and restaurants. The road is almost always being dug up, adding to the hubbub. ✈ *Map M–P6*

1 Central Plaza

Perhaps the developers figured "Central Plaza" had more cachet than "Wan Chai Plaza", or perhaps Wan Chai *is* more central than Central if you're talking about the mid-point of the waterfront. Anyway, this is Hong Kong's second tallest building (after the new IFC Tower) at 374 m (1,227 ft), and has a viewing platform. ✈ *18 Harbour Rd, Wan Chai • Map N5 • 46/F viewing platform 9am–5pm Mon–Fri*

2 Noonday Gun

Immortalised in Noel Coward's famous song about *Mad Dogs and Englishmen*, the famous cannon has been fired at midday each day since 1860. Bigwigs pay for the privilege of firing it, with money going to charity. Otherwise, a gunner dressed in traditional military attire does the honours. Originally it was fired whenever the Taipan arrived or departed from Hong Kong. ✈ *Waterfront near the Causeway Bay typhoon shelter • Map Q5 • To fire gun (for a fee): 2599 6111*

Convention and Exhibition Centre

Left **Happy Valley racing** Right **Hopewell Centre**

5 "Old" Wan Chai

This might soon be labelled Hong Kong's "Little Thailand". Dozens of Thai mini-marts and hole-in-the-wall Thai restaurants have sprung up amid Wan Chai market in the narrow warren of lanes that run between Johnston Road and Queen's Road East. You can find the same dishes here for a quarter of what you'll pay in smart Thai restaurants just blocks away. ◈ *Map N6*

6 Happy Valley Racecourse

From September to June the thud of hooves on turf rings out most Wednesday nights from this famous racetrack – once a malaria-ridden swamp – where Hong Kong's gambling-mad public wager more money per meeting than at any other track in the world. *(See pp12–13.)*

7 Hopewell Centre

Construction mogul Gordon Wu has built roads in China and half-built a railway in Bangkok, but this remains his best-known erection. The 66-storey cylinder rears up behind Wan Chai, making diners dizzy in its revolving restaurant. The food, frankly, is not up to much, but the view

Victoria Park

What Became of Suzie Wong?

Many first-time visitors to Hong Kong have one image of Wan Chai fixed firmly in their heads – that of the Luk Kwok Hotel with its tarts-with-hearts and rickshaw-cluttered surrounds from the film of Richard Mason's novel *The World of Suzie Wong*. It's an image that's at least 40 years out of date. The original hotel was knocked down in 1988, and the soaring glass and steel tower that replaced it, bearing the same name, is full of offices and restaurants. Suzie might still survive, but if she does, she has gimlet eyes and a harridan's scowl.

makes up for it. Nighttimes are most spectacular, or perhaps a cocktail as the sun dips behind the harbour. ◈ *183 Queen's Rd East, Wan Chai • Map N6 • 2862 6166*

8 Victoria Park

Hong Kong's largest urban park opened in 1957, and features a bronze statue of the killjoy British monarch, which one "art activist" once redecorated with a can of red paint. There's a swimming pool, tennis courts and lawn bowling greens. It's also the

Causeway Bay

...enue for the Chinese New Year ...lower Market, and every Sunday ...t noon would-be politicians can ...tand up and shoot their mouths ...ff at the forum. ◈ Map Q–R5

9 Causeway Bay Typhoon Shelter

...arnacle-encrusted hulks and ...own-at-heel gin palaces rub ...unwhales with multi-million ...ollar yachts in this packed haven ...rom the "big winds" that ...egularly bear down on the ...outh China coast. There are ...lso quaint houseboats with ...omely touches like flower ...oxes permanently anchored ...ehind the stone breakwater. The ...mpressive edifice to the left as ...ou look out to sea is the Hong ...ong Yacht Club. ◈ Map Q5

10 Tin Hau Temple

...Not the biggest or best-...nown temple to the Chinese ...ea goddess but certainly the ...host accessible on Hong Kong ...sland. Worth a look if you're in ...he area. This was once the ...aterfront, believe it or not. ...here's usually a handful of ...orshippers burning incense and ...aying respects, although it may ...e packed during Chinese ...estivals. ◈ Map R6

A Day for Exploring

Morning

Start off with a brisk stroll through **Hong Kong Park**, a green haven surrounded on all sides by thrusting towers of glass and concrete. Chances are you'll see several caparisoned couples awaiting their turn to be married at the Cotton Tree Drive Registry Office. Take time for a look through the Edward Youde Aviary, a spectacular creation of mesh arches replete with Southeast Asian birdlife.

Make your way down past Citibank's imposing black towers to **Pacific Place** (see p63) for a coffee and some window shopping. Keep heading towards the harbour and you'll see to your right the elegant sweep of the **Convention and Exhibition Centre** (see p67). Enjoy the harbour panorama through soaring glass walls.

Afternoon

Return to Wan Chai for lunch. **Lockhart Road** (see p67) is as good a place as any. The sleazy joints are still slumbering, and there is decent pub grub, Thai, Mexican and Chinese food on offer (see p71).

Hennessy Road is the place to jump on a tram to Causeway Bay, due east of Wan Chai, or you may prefer to go one stop on the MTR. If you want to go shopping, take the Times Square exit, and start exploring from there. Then leave the crush and chaos behind with a leisurely afternoon stroll through **Victoria Park**, and perhaps a cocktail in Totts, the eyrie atop the Excelsior hotel.

Left **Sogo** Right **Joe Bananas**

 Places to Shop

1 Page One
The best bookshop in Hong Kong, not least because the books are all stacked facing outwards. Huge range of fiction and non-fiction at reasonable prices. ◈ *B1 Times Square, 1 Matheson St, Causeway Bay • Map P6*

2 Jusco
One of Japan's biggest department store chains. Lower rents to the east of the island translate into cheaper fashion, food and household goods. ◈ *Kornhill Plaza 2, Kornhill Rd, Quarry Bay • Map F5*

3 Sogo
With a fine range of mostly Japanese goods, Sogo is very popular among locals, though not up to Seibu's standards *(see p63)* in the hipness stakes. ◈ *555 Hennessy Rd, Causeway Bay • Map P6*

4 Island Beverley
An arcane arcade stuffed with tiny boutiques featuring the creations of talented young local designers. ◈ *1 Great George St, Causeway Bay • Map Q5*

5 Fashion Walk
Lots more interesting boutiques here. The vibe is similar to the Island Beverley. Good place to find bargain cosmetics. Also, check out D-Mop. ◈ *Paterson St, Causeway Bay • Map Q5*

6 J-01
This store is cool bordering on crazy. The highlight of the hip and happening design collection is the "Splatter Collection" by Japanese artist Dehara Yukinori. It's hard to say if he's trying to be comical or is seriously deranged. Either way, don't miss his lurid, twisted figurines such as *Killed Person* and *Brainman*. ◈ *57 Paterson St, Causeway Bay • Map Q5*

7 Mitsukoshi
Another Japanese department store, less swanky than Sogo or Seibu. ◈ *500 Hennessy Rd, Causeway Bay • Map P6*

8 Marathon Sports
Acres of trainers and sporty stuff. ◈ *Shop 616, 6/F Times Square, 1 Matheson St, Causeway Bay • Map P6*

9 Tai Ping Carpets
Lots of lush and lovely rugs. They'll ship them home for you. ◈ *Shop 816, 8/F Times Square, Causeway Bay • Map P6*

10 Lee Gardens
Prada, Paul Smith, Versace, Christian Dior and Cartier for the well-heeled. ◈ *33 Hysan Ave, Causeway Bay • Map Q6*

Price Categories

For a three-course meal for one with half a bottle of wine (or equivalent meal) and extra charges.

$	under HK$100
$$	HK$100–250
$$$	HK$250–450
$$$$	HK$450–600
$$$$$	Over HK$600

Fat Angelo's

🔟 Places to Eat and Drink

1 Tango Martini
Wan Chai's hippest bar has zebra-striped couches, Dean Martin-esque music, the best martinis and martini glasses in town, and classy food. 🚫 3/F Empire Land Commercial Centre, 81-85 Lockhart Rd • Map N6 • 2528 0855 • $$$

2 Time After Time
Tiny bar stuffed full of beautiful people. Good wine selection and great sounds. 🚫 118 Jaffe Rd, Wan Chai • Map N6 • 2865 0609

3 Joe Bananas
Notorious meat market by night, good pub food by day. Avoid at all costs during Rugby 7s week (see p37). 🚫 Cnr Luard and Jaffe Rds, Wan Chai • Map N6 • 2529 1811 • $$

4 Fat Angelo's
Vast servings of pasta. Too many trips here and you'll look like the owner. Bread rolls the size of loaves. 🚫 414 Jaffe Rd, Wan Chai • Map N6 • 2574 6263 • $$

5 Orange Tree Bar and Grill
The latest evidence of Wan Chai's renaissance. Dutch cuisine and wacky modern Dutch art on the walls. 🚫 128 Lockhart Rd • Map N6 • 2866 4545 • $$

6 American Peking Restaurant
Opened in the 1950s and still going strong. The name was a trick to attract US servicemen on leave during the Korean War.

Excellent Peking duck. 🚫 20 Lockhart Rd • Map N6 • 2527 1000 • $$

7 The Old China Hand
A legend in its lifetime, although the ambience is not the same since the walled-up front gave way to trendy glass-panelled doors. Still serves up good pub food and cold beer. 🚫 104 Lockhart Rd • Map N6 • $$

8 Totts Asian Grill and Bar
Totts stands for "talk of the town". It's not, but it does have great fusion food, a sushi bar and panoramic views. 🚫 Excelsior Hotel, Gloucester Rd • Map Q5 • 2837 6786 • $$$

9 Brecht's Circle
Cream of the crop of stylish bar-restaurants around Causeway Bay. The mixed crowd is watched over by pop-art portraits of Hitler, Mao and Mussolini. 🚫 123 Leighton Rd • Map Q6 • 2577 9636 • $$

🔟 Brown
Happy Valley has also been taken over by a host of trendy wine bars and eateries. The décor is, well, brown. 🚫 18A Sing Woo St • 2891 8558 • $$

Left **Giant panda, Ocean Park** Right **Floating Restaurants**

Hong Kong Island – South

DESPITE THE SLOW CREEP OF FLOODLIT HOUSING ESTATES *to the east and west, the south of Hong Kong Island (or "Southside" as everyone calls it) retains more than enough rugged coastline, wooded upland and sequestered beach to startle anyone whose preconception of Hong Kong was wholly urban. Traffic from the city passes through the Aberdeen Tunnel and enters a bright and shiny landscape of golf clubs, marinas and opulent homes. There is good swimming at Repulse and Deep Water bays, and even, at Big Wave Bay, some acceptable surf. Over at Stanley, stallholders set out their coral beads and antique opium pipes, while at isolated Shek O, media types and young commuters snap up beachfront village houses. The Dragon's Back ridge, plunging down the southeast corner, offers some of the island's best walking, with views of the South China Sea.*

🔟 Sights in the South

1. Aberdeen Harbour
2. Floating Restaurants
3. Ocean Park
4. Deep Water Bay
5. Repulse Bay
6. Shek O
7. The Dragon's Back
8. Stanley
9. Ap Lei Chau
10. Chinese Cemetery

Ocean Park

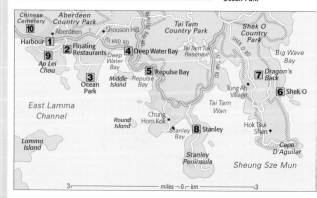

Aberdeen Harbour

good view of the harbour, boats and boatyards. However, when you want to eat, take a ferry from Aberdeen to Lamma Island's many seafood restaurants instead *(see p117)*. ◈ *Map E5*

Aberdeen Harbour
1 Residential blocks crowd Aberdeen's small, lovely harbour, which is still filled with high-prowed wooden fishing boats despite the fact that overfishing and pollution have decimated the Hong Kong fishing industry. Ignore the ugly town centre and instead photograph the tyre-festooned sampans, or walk to the busy wholesale fish market at the western end of the harbour and watch the catches being loaded onto trucks and vans. ◈ *Map E5*

Floating Restaurants
2 Also in Aberdeen Harbour are two giant floating restau-rants, which are popular but garish, production-line eateries. The most famous, The Jumbo, is said to have served more than 30 million people. Prices are not especially attractive, nor are the culinary achievements. Free ferries shuttle between these restaurants, and pushy sampan handlers also lie in wait for meandering tourists. Take one of these boats if you want to get a

Ocean Park
3 This large theme park is Hong Kong's answer to Disney-land, though when Hong Kong gets its own Disneyland in 2005, Ocean Park may seem like a poor relation. In the meantime, there's enough to keep children and adults alike busy for a whole day. Attractions range from rollercoas-ters to giant pandas and great aquatic displays, such as Atoll Reef, which recreates the habitats and sealife of a coral reef *(see also p54)*. ◈ *Map E5 • 2552 0291 • www.oceanpark.com.hk • 10am–6pm daily, to 11pm in high seasons • Adm*

Deep Water Bay
4 There's an almost Mediter-ranean air to the lovely beach and waterfront of Deep Water Bay, a popular place for beach lovers and the well-to-do who settle in the Bay's upmarket housing. The smallish beach is protected by lifeguards and a sharknet, and the water is usually clean. As with most beaches in Hong Kong, it gets crowded in fine weather. ◈ *Map E5*

Left **Fish market, Aberdeen Harbour** Centre **Aquarium, Ocean Park** Right **Deep Water Bay**

Left **Repulse Bay** Right **Shek O**

5 Repulse Bay

Another popular destination, Repulse Bay's beach is clean and well-tended, if sometimes over-crowded with thousands of visitors. Eating and drinking choices range from small cafés on the beach to the Verandah *(see p77)*, a classy restaurant run by the same group as the Peninsula Hotel in Tsim Sha Tsui. Try afternoon tea here. The Hong Kong Life Guards Club at the far southern end of the beach is also worth a look for its scores of statues of gods and fabulous beasts. ◈ *Map F5*

6 Shek O

Remote and undeveloped, the village of Shek O is worth the relatively lengthy train and bus ride necessary to reach it. The serenity is upset only at weekends by droves of sun worshippers heading for its lovely beach. A short walk to the small headland leads to striking rock formations, pounding waves and cooling South China Sea breezes. Surfing and body boarding

House by the sea, Shek O

The Defence of Hong Kong

The British made sure that Hong Kong was well defended from the sea, but it was always vulnerable to attack from the north. During World War II, the island fell to a Japanese attack via the mainland. Hundreds of civilians were interned in Stanley prison, and the well-kept cemetery nearby is the resting place of many who died either trying to defend Hong Kong or during the occupation.

---

are often viable on Big Wave Bay a short walk or taxi ride north. Head to the Black Sheep *(see p77)*, a lovely bar and Mediterranean-style restaurant, for a post-ramble beer and a bite to eat. ◈ *Map F5*

7 The Dragon's Back

This 4-mile (6-km) walk looks daunting on the map, but the route along the gently ascending ridge of the Dragon's Back will not mean too much huffing and puffing for the reasonably fit. The reward is unbeatable views down to the craggy coastline of the D'Aguilar Peninsula, Big Wave Bay and genteel Shek O. At a gentle pace the walk should take about three hours – enough time to build up a good appetite when you arrive in Shek O. Take plenty of water. ◈ *Map F5*

8 Stanley

A former fishing village, Stanley was one of the largest towns on the island before the British arrived and placed a fort on its strategic peninsula. Relics from both eras remain, but Stanley's many excellent seafront restaurants and its extensive market are justifiably the main draws for visitors *(see pp16–17)*.

9 Ap Lei Chau

Supposedly the most densely populated island in the world, Ap Lei Chau (or Duck Island), opposite the Aberdeen waterfront, is crowded with new high-rise developments. Bargain hunters may find a visit to the discount outlets at the southern end of the island worthwhile *(see p76)*. Close to the ferry pier are some small family businesses, boatyards and temples that have survived the modern developments. Ⓢ *Map E5*

Chinese Cemetery

10 Chinese Cemetery

Stretching away on the hill above Aberdeen, the Chinese Cemetery is a great place for photographs, both of the cemetery itself and of the harbour beneath. Negotiating the steep, seemingly endless steps is quite an undertaking, though, especially on a hot day. Ⓢ *Map E5*

A Circular Tour

Morning

This circular tour of Hong Kong Island is perfectly feasible to complete in a day, so long as you don't start too late.

From Central, jump on an Aberdeen-bound bus, alighting close to **Aberdeen harbour** *(see p73)*. Haggle for a sampan harbour tour offered by one of the pushy touts on the waterfront. Don't expect an informative commentary. Keep a look out for Aberdeen's few remaining houseboats.

Avoid the production-line floating restaurants and opt instead for lunch at **Repulse Bay**, which is just a 15-minute bus ride away. Enjoy the beach and a swim, then take lunch either at one of the beachfront cafés or the upmarket **Verandah** *(see p77)*. Alternatively, head to the supermarket behind the Verandah and create your own picnic.

Afternoon

Just a short hop further south along the coast, the lovely town of **Stanley** is certainly worth a visit. If you haven't yet eaten, the restaurants here are excellent, some with lovely sea views. Lose a couple of hours browsing for clothes and souvenirs in **Stanley market**, though admittedly it is not Hong Kong's best market *(see p39)*.

If you want to get some walking in, take a short bus or taxi ride to Tai Tam country park. A path leads through to Wong Nai Chung Gap, from where buses and taxis head back into the city.

Left **G.O.D.** Centre **The Verandah** Right **El Cid**

Designer Outlets in Ap Lei Chau

1 Horizon Plaza
This shabby, high-rise building on the edge of Ap Lei Chau *(see p75)* is home to a number of outlets for discount clothing, warehouse furniture, antiques and home furnishings. A taxi from Aberdeen is probably the simplest way to reach it. ® *2 Lee Wing St, Ap Lei Chau • Map E5*

2 Joyce Warehouse
The extensive selection of clearance designer wear from the stores of Hong Kong chain Joyce are perhaps the main reward for struggling out to Horizon Plaza *(above)*. You get discounts of 60 per cent on the likes of Armani. ® *21/F Horizon Plaza.*

3 Replay
A samples and warehouse shop with limited stocks of casual clothes, but great discounts, often around 80 per cent. ® *7/F Horizon Plaza*

4 Inside
A modest warehouse outlet of a smart interior furnishings chain. There's a small range of clearance items at discounts of up to 90 per cent. ® *16/F Horizon Plaza*

5 The Birdcage
This one offers mostly original Chinese antiques and curios sourced by the owners of the Birdcage shop on the mainland. Items range from portable antiques and curios to furniture. ® *22/F Horizon Plaza*

6 Toys Club
A small shop offering an award-winning selection of educational toys at warehouse prices. ® *9/F Horizon Plaza*

7 G.O.D.
An upmarket chain, G.O.D. ("gee-oh-dee") has some very smart interior goods ranging from furniture to kitchenware, including plenty of items you can fit into your luggage. There are no special discounts here, but it's still worth a nose around. ® *6/F Horizon Plaza*

8 Matahari
Chinese antiques and reproductions, soft furnishings, silk Shanghai-style lamps and hand-painted children's furniture are crammed into Matahari's extensive store and wholesale warehouse. ® *11/F Horizon Plaza*

9 Table Top
Expect discounts of 30–50 per cent at Table Top's small wholesale and export shop. English fine bone china such as Spode, crystal glassware and cutlery are among the offerings. ® *10/F Horizon Plaza*

10 Golden Flamingo
Lots of smaller knick-knacks alongside the bigger-ticket furniture at Golden Flamingo include a wide selection of attractive Chinese vases, picture frames and lacquer jewel boxes. ® *10/F Horizon Plaza*

Price Categories

For a three-course meal for one with half a bottle of wine (or equivalent meal) and extra charges.

$	under HK$100
$$	HK$100–250
$$$	HK$250–450
$$$$	HK$450–600
$$$$$	Over HK$600

Saigon

Top 10 Places to Eat and Drink

1 The Verandah
Indisputably Southside's premier venue, the Verandah, with its candlelight, sea views and old colonial grandeur, is the place for big-budget romancing. *109 Repulse Bay Rd, Repulse Bay • Map F5 • 2812 2722 • $$$$*

2 The Black Sheep
Stroll the quiet lanes of the bohemian enclave of Shek O on the southeast coast, and this veggie-friendly, organic café beckons like a funky oasis. *452 Shek O Village • Map F5 • 2809 2021 • $$*

3 Welcome Garden
Home-style Cantonese cooking of unimpeachable authenticity, served up right by the beach. *770 Shek O Village • Map F5 • 2809 2836 • No credit cards • $$*

4 Hei Fung Terrace
Despite the mall location, this is your safe bet for high-end Chinese dining in Repulse Bay. Come for sublime *dim sum*, then walk it off on the sparkling beach below. *Level 1, Repulse Bay Shopping Arcade • Map F5 • 2812 2622 • $$$$*

5 El Cid
After sangria and tapas on the wide colonial balcony of this upscale Spanish restaurant, Stanley takes on a faintly Iberian edge. El Cid also offers possibly the prettiest views available from the waterfront. *102 Murray House, Stanley Plaza • Map F6 • 2899 0858 • $$$$*

6 Saigon
End a satisfying day in Stanley at this atmospheric Vietnamese restaurant. Romantics will gravitate towards the balcony tables at sunset. *1st floor, 90 Stanley Main St • Map F6 • 2899 0999 • $$$*

7 Tai Fat Hau
With most Repulse Bay restaurants catering to the local millionaire residents, Tai Fat Hau is a budgetary godsend. Late opening (last orders 2:30am) is another plus. *16 Beach Rd, Repulse Bay • Map F5 • 2812 2113 • $*

8 Balcony Café
OK, it's part of a supermarket, but breakfast on this sunny terrace with sea views is one of the Southside's undiscovered bargains. *Park 'N' Shop, Stanley Plaza • Map F6 • 2813 5672 • $*

9 Smuggler's Inn
Stanley's gentrification has thankfully bypassed the Smuggler's Inn, which is a relic of the days when British soldiers from Stanley Fort blew half their wages here. *90A Stanley Main St • Map F6 • 2813 8852 • $*

10 Lucy's
Perennially popular venue for bistro-style nosh, with Mediterranean influences. Vibes are relaxed, standards consistently above-par. Stanley's answer to a light, well-bred lunch. *64 Stanley Main St • Map F6 • 2813 9055 • $$*

Following pages **Plover Cove, the New Territories**

Left **Cultural Centre** Centre **Oysters, Sheraton Hotel** Right **Gargoyle, Boom Bar**

Kowloon – Tsim Sha Tsui

O N ONE LEVEL, *Tsim Sha Tsui (universally truncated to "TST" in a merciful gesture to non-Cantonese speakers) is still a parody of a tourist quarter* in an Asian port: its tailors and camera salesmen do not suffer fools, its hostess bars are the scene of many a ruinous round of drinks. But there is also much more to TST than that. There is a profusion of world-class cultural venues, galleries and museums. There are hotels – the Peninsula, the Inter-Continental, the Great Eagle – of jaw-dropping luxury. And in the monolith that is Harbour City is every product and service the human mind can conceive of.

 Sights in TST

1 The Golden Mile
2 The Peninsula Hotel
3 Museum of History
4 Space Museum
5 Science Museum
6 Museum of Art
7 Kowloon Mosque
8 Cultural Centre
9 Clocktower
10 Kowloon Park

Peninsula Hotel

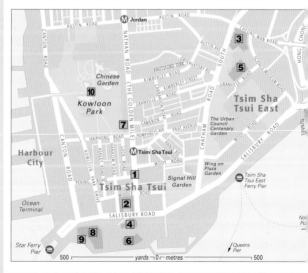

The Golden Mile

The Golden Mile

1 This strip that stretches up Nathan Road from the waterfront could be more accurately dubbed the "neon mile". It's less glitzy than Central and comprises mainly bars, restaurants, tailors, camera and electronic shops and the odd desultory topless bar. The crowds are so great that walking the Golden Mile becomes a major challenge.
• Map N1–4

The Peninsula Hotel

2 The last word in luxury accommodation and service. This venerable hotel sits like a proud old dowager, gazing sedately across at the vertiginous Hong Kong Island skyline. The cheapest rooms start where many other luxury hotels stop, although special offers sometimes apply. A night in the opulent Peninsula suite will set you back the price of a new car. It boasts eight bars and restaurants, including the Philippe Starck-designed Felix and cognoscenti-favoured Gaddi's (see p87). If you desire, you can swoop onto the roof by helicopter. Otherwise you'll be collected by Rolls-Royce. Ⓢ Salisbury Rd, Kowloon • Map N4 • See also p147

Museum of History

3 Brand spanking new and built at a cost of almost HK$400 million. Half of that was spent on its pièce de résistance, the Hong Kong Story, which ambitiously attempts to chronicle the 400 million-odd years since Hong Kong coalesced from the primordial ooze. Controversy lurks, however, in its cursory treatment of the colonial era. The panel of governors' portraits ends at Sir Mark Young, who left in 1941.
Ⓢ 100 Chatham Rd South • Map M3
• 2724 9042 • 10am–6pm daily • Adm

Space Museum

4 When you've had enough of history, come and peek into the future. This odd-looking dome in the heart of Tsim Sha Tsui includes an omnimax theatre and interactive exhibits such as the jetpack ride.
Ⓢ Cultural Centre Complex, 10 Salisbury Rd • Map N4 • 2721 0226 • 10am–9pm Sat, Sun, 1pm–9pm Mon, Wed & Fri. Closed Tue • Adm (free Wed)

Left **Museum of History** Right **Space Museum**

Left **Science Museum** Right **Cultural Centre**

5 Science Museum

Some fascinating interactive displays here if you don't mind fighting your way through the giggling, pushing throngs of schoolchildren. There are enough buttons to push, gadgets to grapple with and levers to tweak to satisfy even the most hard-to-please kids. Basic principles of chemistry, physics, biology and other sciences are explained but in a much more entertaining and less dry manner than in the classroom. ✪ 2 Science Musuem Rd • Map P3 • 2732 3232 • 10am–9pm Sat, Sun, 1pm–9pm Tue–Fri • Adm

6 Museum of Art

You may well be fed up with museums by this point. If not, here you'll find oil paintings, etchings, lithographs and calligraphy. One display features pottery shards and suchlike from southern China dating back to Neolithic times, and there is also a fine collection of elegant porcelain from various Chinese dynasties. ✪ 10 Salisbury Rd • Map N4 • 2721 0116 • 10am–6pm Mon–Wed, Fri–Sun. Closed Thu • Adm (free on Wed)

Museum of Art

Chungking Mansions

This grim and squalid collection of guesthouses, flops and fleapits amid the glitter of Nathan Road has become the stuff of legend over the years, resisting attempts to knock it down. The bottom three floors are full of fabric shops, fast-food joints and lurid video shops. You may trip over a collapsed drug addict in amongst the rats and firetrap wiring.

Hong Kong auteur Wong Kar-wai made this the setting of his 1994 hit film, *Chungking Express*. The best way to experience the Mansions is in one of the cheap Indian restaurants (see p87).

7 Kowloon Mosque

When the muezzin calls the faithful to prayer, the Jamia Masjid Islamic Centre is where you'll find most of Hong Kong's Muslims. You can stop by for a look, but take your shoes off and be respectful. Entry to the inner part is not permitted unless you are a Muslim come for prayer. ✪ 105 Nathan Rd • Map N3 • 2724 0095 • 5am–10pm daily • Jumah prayers every Friday at 1:15pm

8 Cultural Centre

With a peerless view beckoning across the water, the geniuses in charge decided to build the world's first windowless building, and covered it for good measure in pink public toilet-style tiles. Wander around and marvel at one of the great archi-

tectural debacles of the 20th century. That said, it hosts some good dance and theatre.
◈ *10 Salisbury Rd* • *Map M–N4* • *Box office 10am–9.30pm daily* • *2734 2010*

locktower

9 Clocktower

The Kowloon-Canton Railway, which now ends at Hung Hom, used to finish at this clocktower, as did the rather more famous Orient Express *(see also 14)*. Plans are afoot to extend the KCR to Tsim Sha Tsui again by 2003 or thereabouts. From here, you can walk for more than a kilometre around the TST waterfront and marvel at the odd optimistic fisherman dangling a line in the harbour. ◈ *Map M4*

10 Kowloon Park

While in TST, if you feel one more whisper of "Copy watch? Tailor?" may provoke you to irrational violence, then venture through the park gates, find a well-shaded bench and watch the world go by. There's a big swimming pool (reputed to be something of a gay cruising zone), an aviary and a pond featuring flamingos and other aquatic birdlife. ◈ *Haiphong Rd* • *Map M–N3* • *6am–midnight daily*

Kowloon Park

A Morning Out

Early Morning

Catch the **Star Ferry** *(see pp14–15)* to TST. As you come in, check out the vast West Kowloon Reclamation to the left. If the Mass Transit Railway Corporation has its way, a vast tower that will vie for world's tallest building honours will stand here within four or five years.

If you're still standing after the stampede to disembark (be wary of pyjama-clad old ladies), saunter past the old **clocktower**, pause to take in one of the world's most breathtaking views, then cross Salisbury Road and stop for tea at the **Peninsula Hotel** *(see p81)*.

From here, brave the crush and bustle of the **Golden Mile** *(see p81)*. Unless you want a new suit or dress, do not make eye contact with the legion of touts who have never heard the word "no." Walk straight by. They are merciless if they sense weakness.

Brunch

When you've had enough of the smog-shrouded streets, hawkers and being jostled, cross Haiphong Road into **Kowloon Park**. There is plenty of space here to pause and do some serious people-watching.

You'll probably be getting peckish by now. Head back down Nathan Road to Joyce Café, for reasonably-priced vegetarian fare and an earful of *tai-tais* (wealthy housewives) comparing the morning's purchases. The espressos and capuccinos are first-rate; the vegetable lasagna delicious.

Left **Chungking Mansions** Centre **Kowloon Park** Right **Kangaroo Pub**

Spots to People-Watch

The Avenue
Ask for a table near the street, preferably under the glass-roofed section of the restaurant. Floor-to-ceiling plate glass windows provide the perfect vantage point to look down on Nathan Road's passing parade. (Imaginative fusion food, too.) ◉ 50 Nathan Rd • Map N4 • 2315 1118 • $$$

Chungking Mansions
Hours of harmless fun to be had watching the endless stream of freaks, geeks and desperados being accosted by a legion of touts (see also pp82, 87 & 152).

Mirador Mansions
Not as famous as its above-mentioned neighbour, but entertaining nonetheless. More weirdos. More confused backpackers. ◉ 54-64 Nathan Rd • Map N4

Kowloon Park
Best spot is on the benches near the fountain in the centre of the park. In summer, there is a constant and colourful procession along the path (see p83).

Felix
If the wallet won't stand up to a meal, just drink in the bar and watch everyone watching everyone else (see p87).

Harbour City
A people-watcher's paradise. Massive labyrinth of interconnected malls with plenty of cafés and benches to park upon and soak up the orgy of conspicuous consumption (see opposite).

Kangaroo Pub
Try for a seat alongside the windows of this Australian-themed pub and enjoy a cold beer overlooking the entrance to Kowloon Park and its massive banyan trees (see p86).

Planet Hollywood
Only come here to observe the put-upon parents wondering how they got talked into this trip into the dark heart of bad taste and crass commercialism. ◉ Harbour City • Map M3 • 2377 7888 • $$-$$$

Haagen Daaz
A frosty oasis when the mercury soars, with a glass bar and stools to perch upon while you gaze out at the hot and harried shoppers elbowing each other along the Golden Mile. ◉ Cnr Nathan Rd and Peking Rd • Map N

Chaser's Pub
Primo people-watching along groovy Knutsford Terrace, one of Hong Kong's best-kept secrets. ◉ 2-3 Knutsford Terrace • Map N3

Left **Harbour City shopping mall** Right **Joyce**

Places to Shop

1 Harbour City
There are at least 700 shops in this vast agglomeration of malls stretching the length of Canton Road. It comprises the Ocean Terminal, Ocean Centre and Golden Gateway complexes. For serious shoppers only. ◎ *Canton Rd • Map M3–4*

2 Granville Road
Great for souvenir T-shirts, all manner of big label knock-offs and factory seconds. Also top value at chain stores like Bossini and Giordano. ◎ *Map N3*

3 Joyce
Founder Joyce Ma has hit hard times but remains a Hong Kong icon. Her flagship store is in Central, but the Nathan Road outlet is also impressive, particularly if you have a penchant for Prada. ◎ *23 Nathan Rd • Map N4*

4 Rise Commercial Building
It doesn't look much from outside, but within you'll discover a trendsetter's utopia. ◎ *Cnr Chatham Rd South and Granville Rd • Map N3*

5 Beverley Centre
This was the original beacon of cool in TST. Floor after floor of mini-boutiques from young local designers. ◎ *87-105 Chatham Rd South • Map N3*

6 Davidoff
If cigars are your thing, there's an impressive array of stogies here. ◎ *Shop EL3, The Peninsula arcade • Map N4*

7 Star House
Top place for computers, software and all things geeky. Don't be afraid to bargain. ◎ *3 Salisbury Rd • Map M4*

8 Toys 'R' Us
Probably their biggest branch in Hong Kong. Kids will love it, your bank manager may not. ◎ *Shop 032, Ocean Terminal • Map M4*

9 Fortress
If you're after electronic goods and baffled by the sheer number of shops around TST, chain store Fortress is a good bet. Other shops may advertise cheaper prices, but not all dealers are honest. ◎ *Shop 3281, Ocean Terminal • Map M4*

10 Pacino Wan
One of Hong Kong's best-known fashion tyros; the Chinese Vivienne Westwood. Nothing is sacred – not even Her Brittanic Majesty, whose visage can be seen looking most unamused on Wan's lurid creations. ◎ *Shop 2045, Miramar Centre • Map N3*

Left **Schnurrbart** Centre **Oyster Bar, Sheraton Hotel** Right **Morton's of Chicago**

Places to Drink

1 In-V
Upscale bar popular with afflu-
ent tourists and locals alike.
Expect top-notch wines, karaoke
and a cigar divan. ◎ 22 Salisbury Rd
• Map N4

2 Chemical Suzy
Mainly local crowd with a
penchant for Britpop bands, such
as Blur and Oasis. ◎ 2 Austin Rd
• Map N2 • 2736 0087 • No credit cards

3 Bottom's Up
Horribly, horribly sad and
tacky – it featured in James
Bond's *The Man With the Golden
Gun*. Worth a look, just for histo-
rical purposes, of course. ◎ 14
Hankow Rd • Map N3

4 The Bar
On the other hand, 007
would be right at home in this
upscale watering hole. A delightful refuge from the madding
crowds – but prepare to pay
through the nose for beverages.
◎ 1/F The Peninsula • Map N4

5 Kangaroo Pub
"Footy on the telly, mate",
and big slabs of steak on the grill.
Lots of Cathay Pacific pilots
drowning their sorrows here, as
the beleaguered pilots union is
upstairs. ◎ 1/F and 2/F, 35 Haiphong Rd
• Map N3

6 Schnurrbart
German brewing at its
finest, although the delicious
ales on offer take a while to
pour. Perhaps a schnapps while
you wait... ◎ 9 Prat Ave • Map N3

7 Boom Bar
Weird fibreglass gargoyles
line the ramparts, but they are
nothing compared to some of
the oddballs and gangsters
inside. Do not, repeat, do not,
make eye contact. ◎ Cnr Prat Ave
and Chatham Rd South • Map N3

8 Bahama Mama's
A little worn around the
edges, but still the best watering
hole on trendy Knutsford Terrace.
DJs play a range of sounds, there's
table football ("foosball"), surf-
boards and alcoholic slurpees.
◎ 4–5 Knutsford Tce • Map N3

9 Rick's Café
Another spot past its sell-by
date. DJs spinning very commercial tunes, but it's fine for a
dance. ◎ 53-55 Kimberley Rd • Map N3

10 Ned Kelly's Last Stand
This place has been here
forever, as has the jazz band.
Foot-tapping tunes by the
crustiest, most grizzled bunch of
musicians this side of New
Orleans. ◎ 11A Ashley Rd • Map N3

Price Categories

For a three-course meal for one with half a bottle of wine (or equivalent meal) and extra charges.

$	under HK$100
$$	HK$100–250
$$$	HK$250–450
$$$$	HK$450–600
$$$$$	Over HK$600

Gaylord

10 Places to Eat

1 Wine and Oyster Bar
Sublime view and oysters so fresh they flinch when you squeeze a lemon on them. *18/F Sheraton Hotel, 20 Nathan Rd • Map N4 • 2369 1111 • $$$*

2 Felix
The food is fantastic, the view better and the bar crammed with the rich and famous. The highlight, for men at least, are the cheeky Philippe Starck-designed urinals, where you believe yourself against a glass wall and feel like you're showering Hong Kong. *28/F, The Peninsula • Map N4 • 2315 3188 • $$$$$*

3 Morton's of Chicago
Carnivore's paradise. Huge slabs of cow, aged and cooked to perfection. *4/F Sheraton Hotel • Map N4 • 2732 2343 • $$$*

4 Dynasty
Cantonese cuisine at its best. *4/F Renaissance New World Hotel, 22 Salisbury Rd • Map N4 • 2369 4111 ext. 6361 • $$*

5 Balalaika
The décor is more rustic than Russian. Try *piroshkies, borscht* or a cold shot of Stoli. *2/F, 10 Knutsford Tce • Map N3 • 2312 2222 • $$*

6 Gaddi's
Impeccable French cuisine, irreproachable service and famous patrons. Gaddi's has earned its reputation as one of Asia's finest restaurants. *1/F The Peninsula • Map N4 • 2315 3171 • $$$$$*

7 Delaney's
Reasonably authentic Irish menu and great range of draught ales and whiskeys. Lots of dim lighting and cosy nooks. *Basement, 71–77 Peking Rd • Map N4 • $$*

8 Gaylord
This place has been going for almost 30 years. Live Indian music complements rich, delicious curries. *1/F Ashley Centre • Map N3 • 2376 1001 • $$*

9 Chungking Mansions
No hygiene awards here, but it has to be done at least once. Follow the touts into the heart of darkness for one of the best and cheapest Indian meals you've ever had. Safe bets are the Delhi Club, Taj Mahal Club and the unappetisingly named Khyber Pass Mess. *(See also pp82, 84 & 152.) Map N4 • $*

10 Lai Ching Heen
Traditional and avant-garde Cantonese cooking elevated to an art form. *Regent Kowloon, Salisbury Rd • Map N4 • 2721 1211 • $$$$$*

Left **Kowloon waterfront** Centre **Market stall, Reclamation Street** Right **Bird-lover**

Kowloon – Yau Ma Tei, Mong Kok and Prince Edward

GRITTY, PROLETARIAN AND UTTERLY ENGROSSING, *Yau Ma Tei and Mong Kok form a heady segue of karaoke bars, dodgy doorways and street markets before terminating in the more upscale apartments of Prince Edward. If Hong Kong has an emotional heartland, then it is these hectic streets, every paving slab the scene of some delicious hustle. Within living memory there were open fields here, but now all is uncompromising Cantonese ghetto. Come for some of Hong Kong's best shopping, restaurants of rowdy authenticity and a sensuous barrage that will linger in your mind.*

🔟 Sights

1. Bird Garden
2. Flower Market
3. Tin Hau Temple
4. Temple Street
5. Jade Market
6. Ladies Market
7. West Kowloon Reclamation
8. Boundary Street
9. Shanghai Street
10. Reclamation Street Market

Façade detail, Tin Hau temple

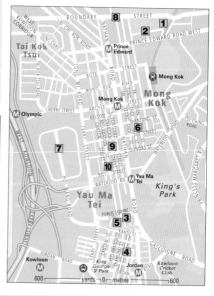

Temple Street

Around Kowloon – Yau Ma Tei, Mong Kok and Prince Edward

88

ird Garden

1 Bird Garden

The small but pretty Bird Garden is where local folk, mostly elderly, take their birds to ing and get some fresh air. here's also a small bird market ere selling sparrows, finches nd songbirds in elegant little ages. Fresh bird food, in the orm of live grasshoppers, is fed o the birds through the cage ars with chopsticks. ⊗ *Flower Market Rd*

2 Flower Market

Near the Bird Garden is a ibrant flower market, at its best nd brightest in the morning. The stalls and shops lining the entire length of Flower Market Road sell a wide variety of exotic flowers – a wonderfully colourful sight and a good place to take photographs. The busy market is especially exciting to visit during the Chinese New Year *(see p36)*. ⊗ *Flower Market Rd*

3 Tin Hau Temple

The Tin Hau temple in Yau Ma Tei is divided into three sections. Only one of these is actually devoted to Tin Hau, the sea goddess who is Hong Kong's favourite deity and essentially its patron. Admittedly, it is neither the oldest nor grandest temple in the territory, but pretty nonetheless. The other two sections are dedicated to Shing Wong, the god of the city and To Tei, the god of the earth. Officially no photography is allowed inside the temple. English-speaking visitors should head for a couple of stalls at the far end of the temple, where they can have their fortunes told in English. ⊗ *Map M1 • 8am–6pm daily*

4 Temple Street Night Market

Visit the chaotic, crowded night market on Temple Street as much for the spectacle as for the shopping *(see pp18–19).*

eft **Flower market** Right **Tin Hau temple**

For more about Hong Kong's markets **See pp38–9**

Left **Quiet lane near Yau Ma Tei's Tin Hau Temple** Centre **Jade for sale** Right **Shanghai Street**

Jade Market

5 The small, covered Jade Market is worth a quick forage even if you're not intending to buy any jade. Dozens of stalls sell jewellery, small animals (many representing characters from the Chinese zodiac) and beads in jade. There will be few bargains on sale, particularly to those without a knowledge of good jade, but there's plenty of cheap jade here if you just want to own some trinkets. ◉ Kansu St
• Map M1

Ladies Market

6 The term "ladies" is somewhat out of date, as there's plenty more than women's clothing here. The shopping area consists of three parallel streets: Fa Yuen Street, crammed mostly with sports goods and trainer shops; Tung Choi Street (the former ladies market); and Sa Yeung Choi Street, specializing in consumer electronics. Market stall prices are cheap, and shop prices are better than those on Hong Kong Island. The crowds can be tiring, though, especially on hot days. ◉ Map E4

West Kowloon Reclamation

7 Currently a pedestrian no-go area, the reclaimed land of West

The Triads

Overcrowded Mong Kok is the heartland of the Hong Kong triad gangs. The triads originated in 17th-century China as secret societies who tried to reinstall the Ming dynasty after the Manchus took over. Though they have been given a romantic image in literature and the cinema, the modern-day reality is of sleaze and slayings. Tourists are unlikely to be a target, however, so don't be put off visiting this exciting district of Hong Kong.

Kowloon is a jumble of road intersections and messy building sites. It will also be the site of what is projected to be the world's tallest building, assuming it goes ahead (see pp42–3). The 480-m (1,575-ft) high Kowloon Station Tower is due for completion in 2006 or 2007 and will cost an estimated HK$20 billion (US$2.56 billion). ◉ Map L1–3

Boundary Street

8 History is visible in the ruler-straight line of Boundary Street, which marked the border between British Hong Kong and China between 1860 and 1898. The lower part of the Kowloon Peninsula was ceded (suppo-sedly in perpetuity) by China to the British, who wanted extra and for army training and commerce. The British then became worried over water shortages and wanted yet more land to protect Hong Kong Island from the threat of bombardment from newly invented long-range artillery. In 1898 the border was moved again to include the entire New Territories, this time on a 99-year lease *(see p30)*. ◈ *Map E4*

9 Shanghai Street

The whole area around Shanghai and Reclamation Streets is a traditional Chinese neighbourhood, if somewhat less vibrant and seedier than it was a few years ago. Interesting nooks and shops include funeral parlours, herbalists, health tea shops, paper kite shops and, at 81 Ning Po Street, a shop selling pickled snakes. ◈ *Map E4*

10 Reclamation Street Market

If you haven't seen a Hong Kong produce market in full swing, you could do worse than wander down Reclamation Street. This predominantly fruit and vegetable market will provide some good photo opportunities. The squeamish, however, may want to avoid wandering inside the municipal wet market building where livestock is freshly slaughtered and expertly eviscerated on the spot. ◈ *Map E4*

Kitchen utensils shop, Shanghai Street

Down the Peninsula

Early Morning

🕐 Take the MTR to Prince Edward to start at the top of the Kowloon Peninsula, near the old Chinese border at **Boundary Street**. Take Exit B2 and head to the **Bird Market** via the flower shops and stalls on **Flower Market Road** *(see p89)*. Testament to the Chinese love of exotic goldfish, the stalls at the top of Tung Choi Street sell a surprising variety of shapes and colours.

Cheap shops and market stalls abound a short walk away to the south on the streets below Argyle Street and east of Nathan Road. Pedestrians also abound – some 150,000 souls live in every square kilometre of this part of the Peninsula.

Crossing Nathan Road, head to the **Jade Market** for jewellery and figurines. If you want the best choice of jade, arrive before lunchtime because some of the stallholders pack up after this.

Early Afternoon

Take a breather in the small, pleasant square across the way and watch the world go by with the elderly locals, or peep inside the busy **Tin Hau Temple** *(see p89)*. Then break for a rough and ready cheap Chinese lunch in the covered canteens on the corner of Pak Hoi and Temple streets.

After lunch explore the produce stalls along **Reclamation Street** and the old Chinese district around **Shanghai Street**.

91

Left **Chan Chi Kee Cutlery** Right **CRC Department Store**

Funky Shops

1 King Wah Building

Uncrowded mall with funky street clothing, accessories, handbags and watches. There's genuine vintage denim and other 70s and 80s rarities, and kitsch Japanese cartoon ephemera aplenty. ◈ *628 Nathan Rd*

2 IT

Smart, minimalist outlet for sleek Japanese and American street clothes and accessories. ◈ *2/F IN's Square, 26 Sai Yeung Choi St*

3 Izzue

Another good place for hepcats and urban warriors to find the right tops and dancing trousers for a night out. ◈ *1/F, IN's Square*

4 Sony Pro Shops

Head to the Sony Vaio, Walkman and Playstation Pro Shops for the latest audio and video gems among Sim City's computer shops. ◈ *Sim City, Chung Kiu Commercial Building, 47–51 Shan Tung St*

5 Mongkok Computer Centre

Not such good deals on computer hardware and software as in Sham Shui Po but convenient for a huge selection of games and accessories. ◈ *8A Nelson St*

6 Sasa Cosmetics

Conveniently located outlet of an extensive Hong Kong chain selling cosmetics of every shade and type at very low prices. ◈ *34 Argyle St*

7 Ban Fan Floriculture

The porcelain and ceramic vases and wicker-work flower baskets may not win awards for chic or design, but the choice is impressive and the prices are reasonable. ◈ *Flower Market Rd*

8 Chan Chi Kee Cutlery

Cheap, sturdy woks, steamers, choppers and pretty much everything else you might desire for the well-equipped kitchen. ◈ *316–318 Shanghai St*

9 CRC Department Store

A good place to head if you are after inexpensive souvenirs such as teapots and ornaments. There's also a well-priced selection of Chinese teas and food. ◈ *Argyle Centre Tower 1, 65 Argyle St*

10 Fa Yuen Building

For audio and video-philes, here is the latest in sleek gadgetry at competitive prices ◈ *75–77 Fa Yuen St*

Price Categories

For a three-course meal for one with half a bottle of wine (or equivalent meal) and extra charges.

$	under HK$100
$$	HK$100–250
$$$	HK$250–450
$$$$	HK$450–600
$$$$$	Over HK$600

Left **Saint's Alp Teahouse** Right **KK Pub & Café**

🔟 Cheap and Chinese Eats

1 Tak Fook Heen
Decent Cantonese food including good, cheap *dim sum*. ◈ B/F, Stanford Hotel, 118 Soy St • 2710 213 • $$

2 Double Congee
Huge bowls of tasty steaming congee (a thick rice gruel or powder with hunks of gristly meat) at this Cantonese canteen. ◈ Shop A, 67 Waterloo Rd • 2624 4173 • No credit cards • $

3 Mui Chai Kee
A great stop for a pot of tea and some fruit jellies and lotus paste buns. The adventurous might try the bird's nest and egg tarts or double boiled frog's oviduct with coconut milk. ◈ G/F, 20 Parkes St • Map N2 • 2388 8468 • No credit cards • $

4 Peking Restaurant
Peking duck is the speciality, or try Yangzhou fried rice with ham and peas at this gently ageing, charming restaurant. ◈ F/F 227 Nathan Rd • Map N2 • 2735 1316 • No credit cards • $$

5 Saint's Alp Teahouse
Quirky snacks and an intriguing menu of teas in a contemporary Taiwan-style Chinese teahouse, part of an extensive chain. ◈ 61a Shantung St • 2782 1438 • No credit cards • $

6 KK Pub & Café
You can't miss this lively place with a cigar-smoking gorilla looming over the entrance. Basic Chinese and Western food, and beer. ◈ F/F, 44-58 Soy Street, Mong Kok • 2388 7115 • $$

7 Ah Long Pakistan Halal Food
A good bet if you fancy a spicy curry, although the surroundings aren't pretty. ◈ G/F, Tak Lee Bldg, 95 Woosung St • Map N2 • 2782 1635 • No credit cards • $

8 Fairwood
Part of a large Chinese fast food chain, this branch has CD listening posts and some Internet terminals. ◈ G/F, King Wah Bldg, 620-628 Nathan Rd • 2302 1003 • No credit cards • $$

9 The Lobby Lounge
Deserves a mention for its glass atrium, quiet outdoor seating, terrific coffee and afternoon tea menus. ◈ 4/F, The Eaton Hotel, 380 Nathan Rd • Map N1 • 2710 1863 • $$

🔟 Light Vegetarian
Familiar mock-meat dishes on the à la carte menu, but the real steal is the ample lunchtime buffet, which includes desserts and a pot of tea. ◈ 30 Jordan Rd • Map N2 • 2384 2833 • No credit cards • $

Note: Unless otherwise stated, all restaurants accept credit cards

Left **Temple prayer sticks and incense** Centre **Rainforest Café** Right **Lion Rock**

New Kowloon

THE SITE OF THE OLD AIRPORT, *Kai Tak has not been allowed to lie fallow with the former terminal converted into the world's largest golf driving range and indoor go-kart track. In the neighbouring streets are excellent budget dining and seconds outlets, for this is where locals go bargain-hunting. Culture is found to the north, in the Tang Dynasty-style architecture of the Chi Lin Nunnery or the joyful chaos of Wong Tai Sin Temple.*

Sights in New Kowloon

1. Wong Tai Sin Temple
2. Lion Rock
3. Kowloon Walled City Park
4. Oriental Golf City
5. Chi Lin Nunnery
6. Lei Yue Mun
7. Karting Mall
8. Lei Chung Uk Tomb
9. Hau Wong Temple
10. Apliu Street

Kowloon Walled City Park

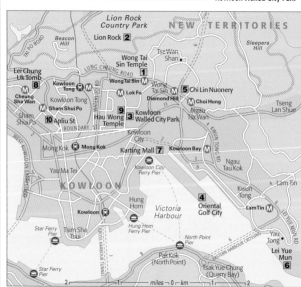

Left **Smoky offerings** Right **Wong Tai Sin Temple**

Wong Tai Sin Temple
1 A noisy, colourful affair, Wong Tai Sin is always crowded and aswirl with incense smoke. Legend holds that Wong Tai Sin (originally known as Huang Chu-ing), who was born in Zhejiang province around AD 328, could see the future and make wishes come true. The temple opened in 1921, after a Taoist priest brought a sacred portrait of Huang to Hong Kong. Its vivid, stylised architecture contrasts sharply with the surrounding concrete boxes. Worshippers from the three main Chinese religions – Taoism, Buddhism and Confucianism – flock here, not to mention 100-odd soothsayers hawking their services. Find out for yourself if they are as accurate as Huang. Behind the temple is an ancient and mysterious tomb that still baffles historians. ◈ Map F4 • 7am–5:30pm

Lion Rock
2 One of the best places to view this fascinating natural landmark is, conveniently, from outside Wong Tai Sin temple. Find the open area near the fortune tellers' stalls where you can look straight up at what from this angle resembles the grizzled head of a male lion. Those feeling energetic may be tempted to scale its heights. Take lots of water, and be warned – the top section is not for the faint-hearted. ◈ Map E4

Kowloon Walled City Park
3 One of Hong Kong's most picturesque parks began life in 1847 as a Chinese fort. A legal oversight by the British left the fort under Chinese control after the New Territories were leased to Britain. It was levelled during World War II, and a labyrinthine ghetto called the Walled City sprang up in its place. This bizarre place quickly became a magnet for triads, drug dealers, heroin addicts, pornographers and rats the size of small dogs *(see p96)*. It was pulled down in 1992 and replaced by the park. A display of photographs in the almshouse near the entrance tells the story. ◈ Map E4

Maze, Kowloon Walled City Park

Oriental Golf City
4 This is, reputedly, the world's biggest driving range, with more than 200 bays. Whack away to your heart's content – unless you're well-connected or seriously rich, this is as close as you'll get to a golf course in Hong Kong. ◈ Kai Tak Runway, Kai Fuk Rd • Map F4 • 2522 2111 • 7am–midnight • Adm

Chi Lin Nunnery

5 Chi Lin Nunnery

It is said that not a single nail was used in the construction of this lavish replica of a traditional Tang Dynasty (AD 618–907) place of worship. The nunnery opened in 2000, funded by donations from wealthy families, whose names are inscribed under the roof tiles. Few original structures survived the Cultural Revolution of the 1960s, so this is a rare chance to see the ingenuity of ancient Middle Kingdom architecture. There are also impressive statues of the Sakyamuni Buddha, ornate gardens and gently whispering waterfalls, and the underlying hum of the chanting, shaven-headed nuns.
◎ Chi Lin Drive, Diamond Hill • Map F4 • 9am–4:30pm daily • Free

6 Lei Yue Mun

Once a fishing village, Lei Yue Mun translates as "carp gate", although the only fish you're likely to see now are in the excellent seafood restau-

The Grimmest Conditions on the Planet

More than 50,000 poor souls once inhabited the Kowloon Walled City *(see p95)*, a place of few laws and no taxes, but plenty of diseases and desperate criminals. In the 1950s the triads moved in, and the narrow lanes often ran red with blood. Before 1992 it was also one of the few places left in Hong Kong to find grizzled opium addicts puffing away in divans.

rants lining the waterfront. This is the closest point between Hong Kong Island and Kowloon but don't be tempted to swim across – if the pollution doesn't kill you, you'll be whisked away by the strong currents. ◎ Map F5

7 Karting Mall

We're talking serious fun here. The old Kai Tak airport departure hall has been transformed into three indoor circuits, making this the biggest indoor go-kart track

Left **Chi Lin Nunnery complex** Right **Lei Yue Mun fish market**

Asia, if not the world. Electric motors accelerate to 35 mph (0 kph) in seconds, which feels ighty fast when you are sitting most at ground level. Roll bars ake these karts safer than their sky outdoor counterparts. ⊗ Map 4 • 2718 8199 • Noon–10pm Mon–Thu, Jam–midnight Fri–Sun • Adm

8 Lei Chung Uk Tomb
The Han burial tomb (AD 24–20) can barely be seen through scratched sheet of perspex. Still, 's one of Hong Kong's earliest urviving historical monuments, o act impressed. ⊗ 41 Tonkin St, ʹham Shui Po • Map E4 • 10am–1pm, pm–6pm. Closed Mon • Free

9 Hau Wong Temple
Quaint and tiny, Hau Wong is ʹardly worth a special trip, but ʹake a look if you're in the area. t was built in 1737 as a ʹnonument to the exiled boy-ʹmperor Ping's most loyal ʹadvisor. Usually fairly quiet ʹunless a festival is in full swing. ⊗ Junction Rd • Map E4 • 8am–5pm daily

10 Apliu Street
This huge street market is ʹfull of all sorts of strange junk ʹand pirated goods. You'll feel ʹyou're on another planet here – ʹthis is as "local" as Hong Kong ʹgets. It includes perhaps the ʹworld's biggest collection of ʹsecondhand electrical stuff. ʹOccasionally you can spot the ʹodd retro turntable or radio, but ʹmost of it is rubbish. ⊗ Map E4

Apliu Street

An Afternoon Out

After Lunch

Catch the MTR to **Wong Tai Sin** *(see p95)* and brave the crowds of earnest worshippers at the temple. Some of the fortune tellers in the nearby stalls speak English. Try to bargain them down to a third or quarter of the price given. Some use numbered sticks, others prefer curved bits of wood known as Buddha's lips.

If you're feeling fit, tackle **Lion Rock** *(see p95)*. It's a demanding climb, but the views are superb. The steep inclines towards the top are for the stout of heart only. Take plenty of water on a warm day.

Kai Tak's **Karting Mall** is a fun alternative, just a 10-minute taxi ride away. Test your skills on three twisting tracks, and check out the real Formula 1 cars on display.

Late Afternoon

By late afternoon you should have worked up an appetite, so take a cab to the seafood restaurants on the waterfront at **Lei Yue Mun**. Watch the sun paint the skyscrapers pink and orange as it sinks into the harbour, while you crack open crabs and munch on giant shrimps, all washed down with wine or an icy Tsing Tao beer.

For a really exceptional view, try the **Tai Fat Hau** restaurant *(see p99)* in Lei Yue Mun. Its dining room is set on stilts over the water, with floor-to-ceiling windows. It is particularly famous for shellfish cooked in spicy wine, deep roasted crab and spicy, fried king prawns.

Left **Dragon Centre** Centre **Page One** Right **Festival Walk shopping mall**

🔟 Places to Shop

1 Golden Shopping Centre
Cheap computer equipment here, and nearby shops have a massive range of VCDs and DVDs. Take care – many are poor-quality pirate recordings. 🛇 *Yen Chow St, Sham Shui Po • Map E4*

2 Dragon Centre
Soaring glassy mall in the midst of Sham Shui Po's grime and dust. Good food hall, computer stuff and a terrifying rollercoaster. 🛇 *Cnr Yen Chow St and Cheung Sha Wan Rd, Sham Shui Po • Map E4*

3 Log-On
The household goods division of the stylish City-Super supermarket chain. Best part of this store is called The Gadget – row upon row of well-designed gizmos for the discerning homemaker. 🛇 *Shop UG01, Festival Walk, 80 Tat Chee Ave, Kowloon Tong • Map E4*

4 G.O.D.
If Log-On has whetted your appetite, proceed to G.O.D. – Hong Kong's coolest household shop, with everything from chainmail cushions to stainless steel chopsticks. Just don't call it "god" (it's "gee-oh-dee"). 🛇 *G/F Shop 27, Festival Walk, Kowloon Tong • Map E4*

5 Lancome
Take your pick from the skin check-up, the 45-minute VIP consultation, or go straight for a one-hour facial in a private cabin. 🛇 *Shop LG2–60, Festival Walk, Kowloon Tong • Map E4 • 2265 8665*

6 Page One
Massive branch of Hong Kong's great bookshop chain. To marks for stacking books with the covers facing outward, saving readers badly kinked necks. Good coffee shop, too. 🛇 *Shop LG1-30, Festival Walk, Kowloon Tong • Map E4*

7 BSC Boutique
For the shopper who has everything… how about a zebra skin toilet seat? Great range of wacky bathroom stuff and gorgeous handmade glycerine soaps in psychedelic colours from Primal Elements. 🛇 *Shop G-31, Festival Walk, Kowloon Tong • Map E*

8 Crabtree and Evelyn
More sweet-smelling goodies to pamper yourself with here. The smell of lavender pot-pourri nearly knocks you over as you enter. 🛇 *Shop LG-220, Festival Walk, Kowloon Tong • Map E4*

9 Bang & Olufsen
Audophiles will drool over the sleek designs and crystal clarity from one of the most distinguished names in sound. 🛇 *Shop LG1-10, Festival Walk, Kowloon Tong • Map E4*

10 Artemis
Great range of shoes, particularly their eponymous label. 🛇 *Shop 139, level 1, Plaza Hollywood, Diamond Hill • Map E4*

Price Categories

For a three-course meal for one with half a bottle of wine (or equivalent meal) and extra charges.	**$** under HK$100
	$$ HK$100–250
	$$$ HK$250–450
	$$$$ HK$450–600
	$$$$$ Over HK$600

...ning at Zen

10 Places to Eat and Drink

1 Combo Thai
Kowloon City is famous for ...s cheap and tasty Thai food. You ...ay need a couple of beers to ...ut out the fire from the beef ...lad. ◉ *14 Nga Tsin Long Rd, Kowloon ...ty • Map E4 • 2716 7318 • $$*

2 Sham Tseng Yue Kee Roast Goose Restaurant
...ocals can't get enough of the ...ewed goose intestines, though ...e less exotic roast goose with ...lt and pepper is a better bet. ...6 Nam Kok Rd, Kowloon City • Map E4 ...2383 1998 • $*

3 Yuet Hing Yuen
Vietnamese is added to Kow-...on City's cosmopolitan blend. ...ot pot, spring rolls and *pho* ...oup can be washed down with ...y Vietnamese 33 beer. ◉ *70–72 ...ja Tsin Wai Rd, Kowloon City • Map E4 ...2382 3282 • No credit cards • $$*

4 Zen
...A calming oasis serving up top-...otch *dim sum*. Roast pigeon ...nd deep-fried duck tongues ...ight suit the adventurous diner. ◉ *Shop G-25, Festival Walk, Kowloon ...ng • Map E4 • 2265 7328 • $$$*

5 Top Banana Club
Serving a buffet-style dinner, ...rill specialities and a great ...election of steaks, this restau-...nt features a rooftop terrace ...ith harbour views. ◉ *6/F Bel Shine ...entre, 40 Nga Tsin Wai Road, Kowloon ...ty • Map E4 • 2382 6065 • $$*

6 Amaroni's Little Italy
Hong Kongers love Italian, and they have taken this place to heart. Share plates and make yourself at home. ◉ *Shop LG1-32, Festival Walk, Kowloon Tong • Map E4 • 2265 8818 • $$*

7 Tso Choi
Literally "rough food", this is one for those prepared to take some culinary risks to experience the real Hong Kong. Are you up to sauteed pig's intestines and fried pig's brains? ◉ *17-19 Nga Tsin Wai Rd, Kowloon City • Map E4 • 2383 7170 • No credit cards • $*

8 Festive China
In fact, the festivities are fairly muted here, but the food is good. Northern-style Chinese cooking and glossy interiors. ◉ *Shop LG-1, Festival Walk, Kowloon Tong • Map E4 • 2180 8908 • $$*

9 Tai Fat Hau
This place juts out over the water at Lei Yue Mun, offering delicious Chinese seafood dishes like shellfish cooked in spicy wine, and grilled king prawn. ◉ *58A Hoi Pong Rd Central, Lei Yue Mun • Map F4 • 2727 4628 • $$$*

10 Kong Lung Seafood
You can't miss this place – two huge stone lions guard the front door. Deep-roasted crab and steamed abalone with orange crust rate highly. ◉ *62 Hoi Pong Rd West, Lei Yue Mun • Map F4 • 2775 1552 • $$$*

Left **Stairs to Ten Thousand Buddhas Monastery** Centre **Railway Museum** Right **Lek Yuen Brid**

The New Territories

AS A NAME, THE NEW TERRITORIES is suggestive of frontier country; in colonial times this was indeed the place where pith-helmeted sahibs went on tiger shoots, threw tennis parties and wrote memoirs. Today, much it is suburban rather than rural: more than a third of Hong Kong's populatio lives here, in dormitory towns dotted across "the NT", as locals abbreviate it. But to the north are Hong Kong's largest expanses of open country, includin the important Mai Po marshes, and there are centuries-old temples and settl ments. At the NT's northern extremity is the border with "mainland" China.

🔟 NT Sights

1 Ten Thousand Buddhas Monastery
2 Sha Tin Racecourse
3 Amah Rock
4 Hong Kong Railway Museum
5 Ching Chung Koon
6 Kadoorie Farm
7 Heritage Museum
8 Yuen Yuen Institute
9 Tin Hau Temple
10 Castle Peak Monastery

Left **Amah Rock** Centre **Racegoer, Sha Tin** Right **Pagoda, Ten Thousand Buddhas Monastery**

Around the Region – The New Territories

...mages, Ten Thousand Buddhas Monastery

Around the Region – The New Territories

track, where record-breaking sums are wagered on Saturday and Sunday afternoons between September and June. Form guides are published in the *South China Morning Post* on race days. ◈ Map F3 • Come Horseracing Tour 2366 3995 • No children • Adm

1 Ten Thousand Buddhas Monastery

he multitude of Buddhas in uestion are stacked on shelves n the main hall of this hillside anctuary at Pai Tau Tsuen, Sha in. In fact, there are more like 3,000 Buddha images now – ou can pity the poor monk who s given the task of counting hem. The monastery comprises ve temples, two pavilions and n elegant nine-storey pagoda. ake a deep breath before you nter the grounds – there are 00-odd steps to negotiate. ◈ Map E3 • 9am–5pm • Free

2 Sha Tin Racecourse

long Kong's most famous orseracing track is at Hong ong Island's Happy Valley *(see p12–13)*, but the people who ve in this part of the world are o mad about horseracing they uilt a second racetrack in the T. More than 85,000 punters ave been known to pack Sha in's $500-million world-class

3 Amah Rock

An odd tower of rocks near Lion Rock Tunnel that when viewed from a certain angle, looks eerily like a woman with a baby on her back, hence the name. Legend holds that the *amah's* husband sailed overseas to find work, while she waited patiently for his return. When a storm sunk his boat, she was so grief-stricken she turned to stone. An alternative interpretation is that the rock was created as an ancient phallic symbol. Take your pick. ◈ Map E4

4 Hong Kong Railway Museum

Tai Po's museum is not really one of Hong Kong's best, but trainspotters will like it. A variety of old coaches sit on tracks outside what used to be the Tai Po Market Station, built in 1913. Inside is a tolerably interesting account of a city that has never gone off the rails. ◈ 13 Shung Tak St, Tai Po Market, Tai Po • Map E2 • 2653 3455 • 9am–5pm. Closed Tue • Free

eft **Sha Tin Racecourse** Right **Hong Kong Railway Museum**

Left **Ritual, Yuen Yuen Institute** Left **Mai Po marshes**

5 Ching Chung Koon

The temple's name means "evergreen pine tree", a symbol of longevity and perseverance. The Koon, a Taoist sect, built the first structure, the Palace of Pure Brightness, in 1961 and has since added myriad pagodas, pavilions and peaceful Chinese gardens guaranteed to lower the blood pressure of even the most stress-soaked individual. There's also vegetarian food and a bonsai collection. ◈ *Tsing Chung Path, Tuen Mun • Map C3 • 7am–6pm daily • Free*

6 Kadoorie Farm

Set up by local moguls Lord Lawrence and Sir Horace Kadoorie in 1951 to provide work for some 300,000 penniless refugees, Kadoorie Farm and Botanic Garden is now a centre for conservation and environmental awareness. It includes a deer haven and butterfly house. Prior booking is essential. ◈ *Lam Kam Rd, Tai Po • Map E2 • 2488 0166 • 9:30am–5pm Mon–Sat • Free*

Heritage Museum

Saving the Sanctuary

The NT's Mai Po marshes *(see p44)* are a world-class site of ecological significance, with more than 60,000 birds stopping here on migratory routes each winter. Kingfishers, herons and cormorants abound, and the marshes are one of the last habitats for the near-extinct black-faced spoonbill and Saunders' gull. Hong Kong's premier birdwatchers' paradise has been the subject of fierce debate and hard-fought battles between staunch environmentalists and developers desperate for scarce new land. The environmentalists, fortunately, have the upper hand. The biggest danger is pollution and industrial waste seeping into the marshes from factories at nearby Deep Water Bay.

7 Heritage Museum

Sha Tin's museum vies with the revamped Museum of History in Kowloon for Hong Kong's best museum honours *(see pp20–21)*.

8 Yuen Yuen Institute

This temple complex is popular with Buddhists, Confucianists and Taoists alike. It's usually full of worshippers, so be respectful. The main building is a replica of Beijing's Temple of Heaven. The notices outside carry the latest soothsayers' wisdom on which

...uen Yuen Institute

...igns in the Chinese horoscope ...re set for an auspicious year. Try ...he cheap and tasty vegetarian ...ood in the Institute's restaurant.
◊ Map E3 • 9am–6pm daily • Free

Tin Hau Temple

9 Hidden away at the far end ...f Clearwater Bay sits the oldest ...urviving of Hong Kong's many ...emples dedicated to the sea ...oddess Tin Hau. It's eerily quiet ...s you make your way down the ...teps, through a verdant patch of ...orest. Inside the temple, huge ...pirals of incense drop ash onto ...cale models of fishing boats.
◊ Sai Kung • Map G3 • Free

Castle Peak Monastery

10 ...he 1-mile (1.5-km) walk from ...he nearby light railway station is ...ard, but this is a nice little ...uting to relieve stress if the ...ustle of Hong Kong is getting to ...ou. Suck in some (relatively) ...resh sea air and let the chanting ...f the monks soothe your soul.
◊ Map B3 • 9am–5pm daily • Free

A Day in the NT

Morning

Take the MTR to Kowloon Tong then switch to the KCR train. Get off at Tai Po Market station, and take the 64K bus or a taxi to Fong Ma Po. This is the home of the Wishing Tree. Buy a red paper plate from a stall, scribble down your wish, then hurl it into the tree. If it sticks, your wish is granted. A gorgeous picture opportunity.

Head back to the KCR, and proceed to Fanling station. Take the 54K bus to Lung Yeuk Tau, start of the **Lung Yeuk Tau Heritage Trail** *(see p104)*. This takes you through the five famous walled villages of the New Territories, built by ancient clans as safe havens from marauding bandits. The walk takes a couple of hours, and provides a fascinating insight into what life once was like in these parts.

Afternoon

Take a bus or taxi back to the KCR, and travel on to Sha Tin KCR station. A short cab ride away is the **Lung Wah Hotel** *(see p109)*, which isn't a hotel anymore, but a restaurant. This eating house has been going strong for more than 50 years, so they must be doing something right.

If you are in Sha Tin on a weekend between September and June, head off to the **racecourse** *(see p101)* for an afternoon of thundering hooves.

On weekdays or out of the racing season, check out Sha Tin's excellent **places to shop** at New Town Plaza *(see p106)*.

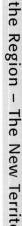

Around the Region – The New Territories

Left **Tsang Tai Uk** Centre **Fish restaurant, Sai Kung village** Right **Ruin, Fanling heritage trail**

TOP 10 Historic Villages and New Towns

1 Tsang Tai Uk
This stronghold of the Tsang clan dates back to 1848 and is built in typical Hakka style, with thick walls and a defensive tower in each corner. Dozens of families still live here. ⊗ Map L3

2 Tsuen Wan
This is the terminus of the MTR line and a perfect example of new town overcrowding. Worth a look just to glimpse Hong Kong life at its bleakest. ⊗ Map D3

3 Sha Tin
Less grim version of Tsuen Wan, with a massive shopping centre. Home to Hong Kong's second racetrack. ⊗ Map E3

4 Fanling
Fanling's Tang Chung Ling ancestral hall belongs to the foremost clan in the New Territories. The Lung Yeuk Tau heritage trail is nearby. ⊗ Map E2

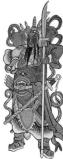

Warrior image, Fanling

5 Sheung Shui
Home to another of the main local clans, the Lius. From here, it's a quick cab ride to Lok Ma Chau, one of the border crossings, where the architects-on-acid skyline of Shenzhen

Kam Tin river

looms through the pall. Another ancestral hall. ⊗ Map E1

6 Sai Kung
Quaint fishing village turned expatriate haunt. Pubs with names like Steamers and the Duke of York, offset by old Chinese men click-clacking mahjong tiles in tiny cafés. ⊗ Map G.

7 Kam Tin
The name means "brocade field", although these days any crops are more likely to be decorated with rusty cars. Traditional walled villages at Kat Hing Wai and Shui Tau. ⊗ Map C3

8 Ping Kong
Off the beaten track, and therefore its walled village is less busy than others. ⊗ Map E1

9 Tap Mun Chau
One of the New Territories' best-kept secrets. Picturesque little island where villagers watch the world go by from quaint homes. ⊗ Map H.
• Ferry 8:30am–6:30pm

10 Tai Po
Its market and Railway Museum are worth a quick look, before making your way to scenic Plover Cove. ⊗ Map E2

Left **Plover Cove** Right **San Mun Tsai floating village**

10 Areas of Natural Beauty

1 Plover Cove
This isn't actually a cove, at least, not any more. In fact it's a massive reservoir which was created by building a dam across the mouth of the bay, then pumping all the seawater out and pumping in fresh water from China. Hike or bike the trails. Maps from HKTB. ✪ *Map F1*

2 Bride's Pool
Stunning waterfalls amid lush forest. Take the camera and wear sensible shoes. ✪ *Map F2*

3 Tai Po Kau
Forest reserve near the Chinese University, popular with serious birdwatchers. ✪ *Map F2*

4 San Mun Tsai
Charming village perched between verdant hills and a sparkling bay. Check out the local fisherfolks' floating homes with their dodgy wiring. ✪ *Map F2*

5 Tai Mo Shan
"Big fog-shrouded mountain" is the translation, although on many days the peak of Hong Kong's tallest mountain is visible. It reaches 957 m (3,139 ft). Quite a hike to the top, but superb views await the intrepid. ✪ *Map D3*

6 Mai Po Marsh
The marsh on the western edge of the New Territories is a bird sanctuary *(see p44)*. ✪ *Map D2*

7 Clearwater Bay
Various walks and beaches on offer here. From Tai Au Mun, you can walk to the less than inspiringly named Clearwater Bay Beach One and Beach Two or Lung Ha Wan (Lobster Bay). Shark sightings send the locals into a lather each summer, and recently holes have been found in some nets. You've been warned. ✪ *Map G5*

8 Long Ke Wan
Relatively inaccessible little gem of a beach. Don't get too carried away with the view as you descend the vertiginous goat track, or you may find yourself at the bottom sooner than you intended. ✪ *Map H3*

9 Tai Long Wan
Hong Kong's finest beach, on the beautiful Sai Kung Peninsula. Take a good map and lots of fluids before setting off *(see pp22–3)*. ✪ *Map H3*

10 Ma On Shan
The mountain's name means "saddle", a reference to its shape *(see p45)*. ✪ *Map F3*

Tai Long Wan

Left **Dickson Warehouse** Right **Universal Models**

Places to Shop

1 Dickson Warehouse Clothing

Genuine bargains here on a host of top designer names. Up to 70 per cent off Polo Jeans, Polo Sport, Ralph Lauren, Guy Laroche, Joan & David and Charles Jourdan. ✆ *Shop 417–18, 4/F, New Town Plaza, Sha Tin • Map E3*

2 My Jewellery

Innovative designs and prices that won't break the bank. Check out their diamond-studded chokers. ✆ *Shop 15, Sha Tin KCR station • Map E3*

3 Universal Models

Plenty here for the model enthusiast, whether you're after incredibly detailed military figurines or the latest Mobile Set Gundam. Scary range of pellet-firing replica guns. ✆ *Shop A315, 3/F New Town Plaza, Sha Tin • Map E3*

4 Yamano

Swanky Japanese cosmetic house. Lotions and potions galore. ✆ *Shop 371, 3/F, New Town Plaza, Sha Tin • Map E3*

5 A&P Service Centre

The weekend warrior's one-stop shop. Some odd-bods in here, gazing lovingly at massive bowie knives and camouflage trousers. ✆ *Shop A329, 3/F, New Town Plaza, Sha Tin • Map E3*

6 Suzuya

Cute, girly Japanese fashion label. Just the ticket if you want to look like Sailormoon. ✆ *Shop 457–9, 4/F New Town Plaza, Sha Tin • Map E3*

7 Bossini

Big branch of the cut-price chain store. Stock up on comfy cotton T-shirts, socks and khakis ✆ *Shop 318–19, 3/F, New Town Plaza, Sha Tin • Map E3*

8 Marks & Spencer

Sensible shoes, comfortable underwear and comfort food for homesick Britons. One of their biggest Hong Kong branches. ✆ *Shop 329–39, 3/F, New Town Plaza, Sha Tin • Map E3*

9 Hang Heung Bakery

Hong Kong's most popular baker of "wife cakes", a flaky pastry filled with red bean paste. These traditional confections are *de rigueur* at Chinese weddings. ✆ *64–6 Yuen Long Main St • Map C2*

Children outside Bossini

10 Wing Wah Bakery

Hong Kong's premier purveyor of moon cakes *(see p50)*. These rich glazed pastry treats are eaten during the Mid-Autumn festival The egg yolks in the centre represent the full moon. ✆ *86 Yuen Long Main St • Map C2*

eft **Shoppers, New Town Plaza** Centre **Cocktails, Pimento Lounge** Right **Regal Riverside Bar**

10 Places to Drink

1 Steamers
Make merry at Sai Kung's nost stylish pub, a big mprovement on the dingy, vindowless Newcastle Pub of its ormer life. Great for people-vatching. *A2-3 Kam Wah Building, 18–32 Chan Man St, Sai Kung • Map G3*

2 Beach Pub
Overlooking the bay and a 10-minute stroll around the waterfront from Sai Kung Town. The Beach Pub has bands on the veekends and a regular crowd of ocal Chinese and expatriates. *Beach Resort Hotel, 1780 Tai Mong Tsai Rd, Sai Kung • Map G3*

3 Railway Tavern
A welcome little watering hole near the Railway Museum n Tai Po. Just the ticket after a hard day's rural meandering. *Tai Po Market KCR station • Map E2*

4 Poets
Don't let the name fool you. Loud discussions about the previous night's Premier League soccer matches are more likely than pompous declamations in ambic pentameter. *G/F 55 Yie Chun St, Sai Kung • Map G3*

5 Duke of York
A Sai Kung institution. A faithful crowd of regulars can be found every night and weekend propping up the bar of this renovated boozer. Very good pub grub, too. *42–56 Fuk Man Rd, Sai Kung • Map G3*

6 Cheers Sports Bar and Restaurant
Another of the new-ish spots that have sprung up in vibrant Sai Kung Town. It's more sophisticated than some of its competitors, but rather boisterous if the soccer or rugby are on the television. *28 Yi Chun St, Sai Kung • Map G3*

7 Regal Riverside Hotel Bar
Up-scale watering hole overlooking Sha Tin's Shing Mun River. A good retreat after a shopping marathon in New Town Plaza. *1/F Regal Riverside Hotel, Tai Chung Kiu Rd, Sha Tin • Map E3*

8 Royal Park Hotel Lounge Bar
One of Sha Tin's many hotel bars. Reasonably priced beers but not much atmosphere. *G/F Royal Park Hotel, 8 Pak Hok Ting St, Sha Tin • Map E3*

9 Kowloon Panda Pimento Lounge
No pandas, but you'll find pimentos in the martinis. Cheap-ish drinks and a decent view over the hills and housing estates of Tuen Mun. *13/F Kowloon Panda Hotel, 3 Tsuen Wah St, Tsuen Wan • Map D3*

10 Kowloon Panda Lobby Lounge
If you can't be bothered getting in the lift, there's another decent bar in the hotel's third-floor lobby. Cheap snacks and beverages. *See previous listing*

Left **Cosmopolitan Curry House** Centre and Right **Chianti Ristorante Italiano**

Cheap Eats

1 Pepperoni's
One of the first decent Western-style restaurants in Sai Kung and still going strong. Huge servings, relaxed ambience. Excellent pizza, pasta, nachos, calamari and a good wine selection. ◈ *18B Main St, Sai Kung • Map G3 • 2792 2083 • $$*

2 Cosmopolitan Curry House
This place has been thriving for years. Cheap, cold beer and spicy Malay and Indonesian curries. Queues to get in are a common sight. ◈ *80 Kwong Fuk Rd, Tai Po • Map E2 • 2650 7056 • $$*

3 Hello Kitty Café
After flooding adolescent bedrooms all over Asia with her useless junk, Hello Kitty has turned her attention to food. Never mind that she doesn't have a mouth. ◈ *1/F Luk Yeung Galleria, 22-26 Wai Tsuen Rd, Tsuen Wan • Map D3 • 2414 3262 • $*

4 Nice Hoover Hot Pot
Cheap Chinese food near the border of mainland China. Best *dim sum* in Fanling – not that there's much competition. ◈ *G/F Comfort Court, 2 Luen Chong St, Luen Wo Hui, Fanling • Map D2 • 2682 0683 • $*

5 Sun Ming Yuen Seafood
Excellent-value *dim sum* and other unpretentious Chinese food in a historic village setting. ◈ *105 Wo Tai St, Luen Wo Hui, Fanling • Map D2 • 2677 8218 • $*

6 Yokel Cook
You might expect grits and fried catfish with a name like this, but in fact it's a mix of Western and Japanese food. ◈ *Shop 210, Plover Cove Garden, Tai Po • Map E2 • No credit cards • 2654 7981 • $*

7 Chianti Ristorante Italiano
Stuff yourself with cut-price pasta at the buffet and marvel at the mediocre service. ◈ *3/F Kowloon Panda Hotel, 3 Tsuen Wah St, Tsuen Wan • Map D3 • 2409 3226 • $-$$*

8 Shalimar
Cheapest curries outside Chungking Mansions. ◈ *127 Kwong Fuk Rd, Tai Po • Map E2 • No credit cards • 2653 7790 • $*

9 Luen Yick Restaurant
Minced pigeon always popular here, along with other Cantonese standards. Charming rural surrounds. ◈ *Luen Yick Village, Sam Mun Tsui, Tai Po • Map E2 • No credit cards • 2664 0455 • $*

10 Shaffi's Indian
The owner is famous in these parts as the former chef for many years for British and Gurkha troops at Shek Kong barracks. After the Handover, he hung out his shingle in Yuen Long – where his faithful fans still seek out his top curries. ◈ *14 Fau Tsoi St, Yuen Long • Map C2 • 2476 7885 • $*

  Note: Unless otherwise stated, all restaurants accept credit cards

Price Categories

For a three-course meal for one with half a bottle of wine (or equivalent meal) and extra charges.	**$** under HK$100
	$$ HK$100–250
	$$$ HK$250–450
	$$$$ HK$450–600
	$$$$$ Over HK$600

Royal Park Chinese

🔟 Restaurants

1 Jaspa's
Good fusion food, friendly staff and lots of antipodean wines at reasonable prices. ◈ 13 Cha Tsui Path, Sai Kung • Map G3 • 2792 6388 • $$$

2 Tung Kee Restaurant
Point at what you want from the huge range of sea creatures swimming in waterfront tanks and haggle a bit. They bag it; you take it to the kitchen; they cook it; you enjoy one of the best seafood meals in Hong Kong. ◈ Shop 11–15, Siu Yat House, Hoi Pong Sq, Sai Kung • Map G3 • 2791 9312 • $$$

3 Lung Wah Hotel
The hotel is long gone, but the pigeon restaurant has been going strong for 50 years. Don't worry that you're eating an airborne rat – the meat is lean and delicious. Occasional celebrity sightings. ◈ 22 Ha Wo Che St, Sha Tin • Map E3 • 2691 1594 • $$

4 Royal Park Chinese
Classy Cantonese cooking – not an easy thing to find in Sha Tin. Specialities include shark's fin soup and crispy chicken. ◈ 2/F Royal Park Hotel, 8 Pak Hok Ting St, Sha Tin • Map E3 • 2694 3939 • $$$

5 Ristorante Firenze
Generally packed, and when you try their pastas washed down with well-priced red wines you'll know why. Good pizza too. ◈ 60 Po Tung Rd, Sai Kung • Map G3 • 2792 0898 • $$-$$$

6 Kar Shing Restaurant
There are few reasons to go to Yuen Long, but if you find yourself there, try Kar Shing's traditional New Territories Great Bowl Feast. Four people will struggle to finish this steaming pile of meat, seafood and vegetables. ◈ 3/F 249 Castle Peak Rd, Yuen Long Plaza • Map C2 • 2476 3228 • $$$

7 Thai-Malaysian Restaurant
Far-flung curry emporium in Sheung Shui. Famed locally for spicy concoctions involving crabs, fish, king prawns and other fruits of the sea. ◈ 28-30 Sun Fat St, Sheung Shui • Map E1 • 2673 2230 • $$

8 Tapas Tree
Candles, spanish guitars, lashings of terracotta. The tapas selection may not please purists but will satisfy the hungry. ◈ Shop 10A, Po Tung Rd, Sai Kung • Map G3 • 2792 6608 • $$-$$$

9 Kaga
Good sushi in Sha Tin. ◈ Shop A191-193, 1/F New Town Plaza Phase 3, Sha Tin • Map E3 • 2603 0545 • $$$

🔟 Baanthai
The restaurant may be in an uninspiring setting in Sha Tin's sprawling New Town Plaza, but the spicy Thai delicacies on offer are just the thing to revive footweary shoppers. ◈ Shop A172, 1/F New Town Plaza, Sha Tin • Map E3 • 2609 3686 • $$-$$$

Left **Tai O** Centre **Lamma Island** Right **Lobster**

Outlying Islands

HONG KONG IS THOUGHT OF *as a city not an archipelago, but there are 260 islands in the group and, assuming you can haul yourself out of the downtown bars and boutiques, some of Hong Kong's most sublime experiences await you there. Now that it is connected to the city by bridge, the largest of the islands, Lantau, is losing the quirky languor it once had; but the smaller islands offer plenty of compensations. From the narrow lanes of Cheung Chau to the outdoor raves of Lamma's Power Station Beach, Hong Kong's islands give you many opportunities to lose yourself.*

🔟 Sights in the Outlying Islands

1. Lantau – Mui Wo
2. Lantau – Tai O
3. Lantau – Sunset Park
4. Lantau – Trappist Monastery
5. Lamma – Sok Kwu Wan
6. Lamma – Yung Shue Wan
7. Po Toi
8. Tap Mun
9. Peng Chau
10. Cheung Chau

Left **China Bear Pub, Lantau** Right **Sunset Peak, Lantau**

Stilt houses, Tai O

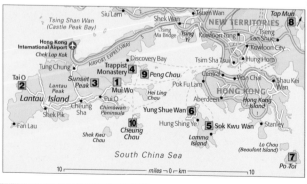

Mui Wo beach, Lantau Island

1 Lantau: Mui Wo

The main ferry from Hong Kong Island to Lantau docks at Mui Wo, or Silvermine Bay as the British named it. It's a good starting point from which to explore the island, though not the most beautiful spot on Lantau. Most of the restaurants and bars and a supermarket are just around the corner from the ferry pier. There is also a beach five minutes' walk to the northeast. Enjoy a beer and a game of snooker or stock up for a picnic before walking or beachcombing. ◈ Map C5

2 Lantau: Tai O

Lying on the far western coast of Lantau, the pretty village of Tai O is a trek from Mui Wo but it's worth the effort. Sitting in a tidal estuary, this is one of the last places in Hong Kong where you can see the traditional stilt housing of southern Chinese fishing villages. Some are as small as dolls' houses. For an authentic Hong Kong consumable, buy a jar of shrimp paste, a powerful type of fish sauce created by fermenting shrimp and spices in a barrel in the sun. It's actually much better than it sounds. ◈ Map A5

3 Lantau: Sunset Peak

For the reasonably fit, Sunset Peak offers the finest views on Lantau. The 934-m (3,063-ft) high mountain, Hong Kong's second highest, commands great views across Hong Kong, down onto the international airport, Po Lin Monastery and the lovely wooded valleys of this sparsely inhabited terrain. Hardy souls stay at the nearby Youth Hostel and head up the peak for Hong Kong's most spectacular sunrise. Obviously all this only applies in clear conditions. ◈ Map B5

4 Lantau: Trappist Monastery

The chapel, next to a dilapidated old dairy farm, is open to visitors willing to observe the silence of the monastery. Apart from that, there's not much to see at the monastery itself, but it's a good excuse for a gentle woodland walk to or from Discovery Bay. The monastery is also served by a ferry pier with infrequent Kaido services to Discovery Bay and the island of Peng Chau (see p115), which has many seafood restaurants. ◈ Map C5 • Free

Tai O fishing village

For Lantau's Big Buddha and Po Lin Monastery See pp28–9

Peng Chau harbour

5 Lamma: Sok Kwu Wan

Don't expect many sights in Lamma's main area of development on the east coast. Sok Kwu Wan is known mainly for its quarry and wall-to-wall seafood restaurants along the harbour front. The seafood tanks are a sight in themselves, however, with some monster-sized fish and crustaceans. There's not much to differentiate most restaurants, although the standard is generally very good. Have a look at the pretty Tin Hau Temple at the end of the main street. The lovely 3-mile (5-km) circular walk to the sleepy, remote village and beach at Yung Shue Ha is recommended for the reasonably fit. ◈ Map E6 • Regular ferries from Hong Kong Island

6 Lamma: Yung Shue Wan

Lamma's western coast also has a harbour, with lots of bars and eating choices along the village's endearingly ramshackle main street. Watch villagers, resident expats and fellow visitors wander by, before hitting the well-kept beach at Hung

Lantau's Pink Dolphins

The rare and endangered dolphins of the Pearl River Delta can usually be found at play near the coast of Lantau. A guided boat trip to see them is certainly worthwhile. Learn about the lives of these creatures and the threats they face, including pollution, overfishing and lethal boat propellers and hydrofoils. Tours leave at least four times a week (see pp54 &145).

Shing Ye, a 20-minute walk to the southwest. ◈ Map D5 • Regular ferries from Hong Kong Island

7 Po Toi

Getting to this craggy, barely inhabited outcrop of rock south of Hong Kong Island is a logistical challenge (without a hired junk only feasible on Sundays). It's worth the effort, however, for secluded walks and spectacular cliff views over the South China Sea, rounded off with a meal at the island's only restaurant, the Ming Kee (see p117). ◈ Map F6 • Ferry to and from St Stephen's Beach, Stanley, on Sundays

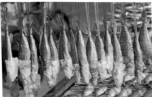

Left **Drying fish** Right **Beach at Hung Shing Ye, Lamma**

For Hong Kong Island's outlying islands ferry piers See Map L4

shermen

8 Tap Mun

To the north of the Sai Kung Peninsula, tiny Tap Mun, which means "grass island", is another remote destination with only a couple of daily connections with the mainland. The rewards are striking rock formations, pounding seas, a herd of cattle and relative seclusion. The island's Tin Hau Temple is surprisingly large and beautiful. Take a picnic, as there are few eating opportunities. Nor is there any accommodation on the island, so be sure to catch that last ferry. ◎ Map H2 • Ferries from Wong Shek and Ma Liu Shui

9 Peng Chau

This tiny island nestling off the coast of Lantau, opposite Discovery Bay, remains in many ways a traditional Hong Kong coastal community. You wander among its narrow alleys, tiny shops and temples to the gentle soundtrack of a distant game of mahjong or the sound of Cantonese opera leaking from an old radio set. But there's no beach, and few eating choices, though the seafood is cheap. ◎ Map C5 • Ferries from Hong Kong Island and Lantau's Discovery Bay

10 Cheung Chau Island

This former pirate haven retains much of its traditional character, from the small-scale shipyards at the harbour's edge to the old temples and shrines that dot its narrow alleys. With many of its inhabitants still being fishermen, it's a good destination for cheap seafood. There are also a couple of excellent beaches (see pp24–5).

A Day on Lantau

Morning

Make a reasonably early start for Lantau from the outlying islands ferry terminal on Hong Kong Island. After disembarking at **Mui Wo** (see p113), take the No.1 bus from outside the ferry pier all the way to its terminus at the old fishing village of **Tai O** (see p113) on the far northwestern coast.

Take in the sights and smells of this ancient settlement before heading back along the road to Ngong Ping for the **Big Buddha and Po Lin Monastery** (see pp28–9).

Have a vegetarian lunch at the monastery, or take a picnic. The area around Ngong Ping is great for gentle rambles with a view and some serious hill climbing (Lantau Peak).

Afternoon

If time still permits, take the bus back towards Mui Wo, but jump out at the fantastic, clean and usually deserted beach at Cheung Sha (ask the driver to let you know when). Spend a relaxed afternoon paddling, swimming and sun-bathing on this glorious stretch of golden sand.

Slake your afternoon thirst and tea-time hunger at **Stoep** (see p117), which offers Mediterranean-style and South African food.

From here it's a short ride back into Mui Wo. Before catching the return ferry, squeeze in a drink at the Hippo or **China Bear** (see p117), two convivial bars near the ferry pier.

Left **Big Buddha** Centre **Boats, Lantau** Right **Hakka woman**

🔟 Photo Opportunities

1 Big Buddha on Lantau
The dramatic setting in itself is worth a picture, let alone the mighty Buddha *(see pp28–9)*.

2 Any Ferry Aft Deck
Gain some perspective on the dramatic skyline of the islands. The Star Ferries offer the best chance to capture the dramatic skyscrapers *(see pp14–15)*.

3 Hatted Hakka Women
The large woven hats draped with a black cotton fringe come from the Hakka people, once a distinct ethnic group in the region. Many women wear these hats around Hong Kong, though not all wearers are ethnic Hakka.

4 Cheung Chau Harbour
Handsome high-prowed fishing boats, squat sampans and busy boatyards are just some of the sights *(see pp24–5)*.

5 Tai O Village, Lantau
The old fishing village on the remote northwest coast is the last settlement in the territory with a significant number of stilt houses, some almost as small as play houses *(see p113)*.

6 Miniature Fire Engine and Ambulance, Cheung Chau
Walk to the northern end of She Praya Road on Cheung Chau Island and peep inside the vehicle bay where you'll see the island's mini-ambulance and tiny fire tender. These toy-size vehicles are designed to navigate the island's narrow lanes.

7 Lamma Restaurants' Seafood Tanks
The restaurants display the subject of their menus live and swimming in huge outdoor fish tanks. You'll see some edible leviathans here from monster grouper to giant lobsters and an absorbing array of other fidgeting crustacea and teeming sealife.

8 View of Airport from Lantau Peak
Take a powerful lens on a clear day to get decent shots of the airport from Lantau Peak. The summit also offers terrific views down onto the monastery and surrounding country. ◈ *Map B5*

9 Hong Kong Airport Planespotters Platform
There's no official viewing area at the airport, so take a taxi or walk to the small hill (the only natural part of this man-made island) just opposite Tung Chung town. There's a footpath to the summit and its pagoda. ◈ *Map B5*

🔟 Tsing Ma Bridge Lookout Point
If big construction projects move the earth for you, then head to the free Airport Core Programme Exhibition Centre in Ting Kau. The viewing platform on the roof offers a great opportunity to photograph the elegant Tsing Ma and Ting Kau bridges. ◈ *Map D3*

Price Categories

For a three-course meal for one with half a bottle of wine (or equivalent meal) and extra charges.

$	under HK$100
$$	HK$100–250
$$$	HK$250–450
$$$$	HK$450–600
$$$$$	over HK$600

China Bear

10 Places to Eat and Drink

1 China Bear, Lantau
Missed the ferry? Never mind. Nip round the corner for one of the cheap lunch specials and a beer micro-brewed on China Bear's premises. ◎ *Mui Wo centre • Map C5 • No credit cards • $$*

2 Stoep, Lantau
Good Mediterranean and South African fodder on one of Lantau's loveliest beaches. Try the tapas-style dishes or the cold Cape-style curried fish. ◎ *32 Lower Cheung Sha Village • Map B6 • 2980 2699 • $$*

3 The Gallery, Lantau
A cosy place with al fresco dining close to a decent beach. The cuisine is Mediterranean and Turkish but dedicated carnivores can choose ostrich and spicy boerewors, a long South African sausage. ◎ *Tong Fuk Village, South Lantau Road • Map B6 • 980 2582 • Closed Mon • No credit cards • $$*

4 Jo Jo, Lantau
Most other restaurants in Discovery Bay are pretty bland, but Jo Jo is a fine Indian eatery. ◎ *Shop 101, 1F, Block A, Discovery Plaza • Map C5 • 2987 0122 • $$*

5 Rainbow Seafood, Lamma
One of Lamma's better places for a full seafood splurge with a harbour view. The locals love it, and so will you. ◎ *16-20 First Street, Sok Kwu Wan • Map E6 • 2982 8100 • $$*

6 Deli Lamma, Lamma
A favourite haunt of local ex-pats and the place for all-night Typhoon parties, the friendly Deli also serves a decent Western and Indian menu. The vindaloos are quite something. ◎ *36 Main Street, Yung Shue Wan • Map D5 • 2982 1583 • $$*

7 Bookworn Café, Lamma
This place wears its ethical, veggy heart on its sleeve, with its twee slogans to peace, love and tofu on its walls. Don't be put off. Service is friendly; the fresh food and juices exceptional. ◎ *79 Main Street, Yung Shue Wan • Map D5 • 2982 4838 • No credit cards • $$*

8 Han Lok Yuen, Lamma
Take a gentle 20-minute walk from Yung Shue Wan for legendary pigeon specialities. Former governor Chris Patten and comedian John Cleese are fans. ◎ *16-17 Hung Shing Ye • Map D5 • 2982 0680 • No credit cards • $$*

9 Cheung Kee, Cheung Chau
Somewhat shabby premises, but the noodles are fresh and the dumplings and wontons just right. There's no signage in English but it's easy to find, just by the ferry pier. ◎ *83 Praya St • Map C6 • 2981 8078 • No credit cards • $*

10 Ming Kee Seafood, Po Toi
Run by a restaurateur and his seven daughters, this is Po Toi's only restaurant. Reach it by junk or from Stanley on a Sunday (see p114). ◎ *Tai Wan • Map F6 • 2849 7038 • No credit cards • $$*

Left **Guia Lighthouse** Centre **Relief, Maritime Museum** Right **São Domingo**

Macau

GAMBLING IS INDISPUTABLY MACAU'S MAIN SCENE, *catering mainly to overnight punters coming by boat or helicopter from Hong Kong. However, this former Portuguese colony is thankfully capable of more than shoddy imitations of Vegas. The Portuguese had 400 years of rich history here, and there are squares of impressively Iberian character if you know where to find them. The indigenous cuisine, fusing Chinese and Portuguese elements, is another draw.*

🔟 Sights in Macau

1. Avenida da Praia Grande
2. Guia Lighthouse
3. Ruinas de São Paulo
4. Largo de Senado
5. Cultural Centre
6. Protestant Cemetery
7. Camões Grotto
8. Forteleza do Monte
9. Dom Pedro Theatre
10. St Joseph's Seminary

Lou Lim Ieoc Garden

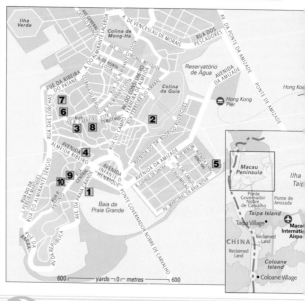

inas de São Paulo

Avenida da Praia Grande

...e graceful boughs of banyan ...ees stretch over this elegant ...enue, shading the candy-...loured pageant of colonial-era ...chitecture. Unlike in Hong Kong, ...any of Macau's historic piles ...rvive in excellent condition. At ...e gorgeous fort-turned-hotel at ...acau's tip, the Pousada de São ...ago, the road becomes Avenida ...Republica. Follow it around ...e point, where it turns into Rue ...Barra and ends in the Porto ...terior (Inner Harbour).

Guia Lighthouse

This most visible of Macau's ...ndmarks has kept its lonely ...gil on Guia Hill since 1638, its ...shing beacon beckoning to ...eryone from Portuguese ...aders to ferocious pirates and ...arauding Dutch navy boats. ...tch the cable car up the hill, ...ke in the 360-degree panorama from Macau's highest point and enjoy a leisurely stroll back down. ◈ Free

3 Ruinas de São Paulo

The façade and intricate mosaic floor are all that remain of Macau's grandest church, perched some-what precariously atop a steep flight of stone steps and propped up by steel scaffolding. In its heyday, the Jesuit-designed Cathedral was hailed as the greatest monument to Christianity in the East. It caught fire during a massive typhoon in 1835, and as the years took their toll, only extensive structural work in the early 1990s stopped the façade from crumbling to rubble. ◈ Free

4 Largo de Senado

Brightly painted colonial buildings and slightly psychedelic paving makes this square in the heart of Macau a favourite with photographers. At one end sits the Leal Senado, or Loyal Senate, now the seat of the municipal government but once the Portuguese headquarters. It was thus named because Macau refused to recognise the 17th-century Spanish occupation of Portugal. ◈ Leal Senado 9am–9pm daily • Free

...ft Food stalls Right Largo de Senado

For entry requirements to Macau See p136

119

Left **Camoes Grotto** Right **Floating Casino**

5 Cultural Centre

This elegant building was designed and put up in time for the December 1999 Handover to China. In fact, the actual ceremony took place behind the centre in a temporary structure designed to look like a giant Chinese lantern. The centre is the focal point for the Macau Arts Festival each March. The only mystery is why there is what appears to be a ski-jump on the roof. ✎ *11am–7pm daily • Free*

6 Protestant Cemetery

Headstone

More interesting than it sounds – indeed, you might find yourself spending hours wandering this grave-dotted grove, reading inscriptions to plague-doomed sailors and colonial adventurers. Those at rest include painter George Chinnery (the Mandarin Oriental's bar in Hong Kong is named after him) and Robert Morrison, the first Protestant to venture to China in search of converts. ✎ *9am–6pm daily • Free*

7 Camões Grotto

The author of the 16th-century Portuguese epic *The Lusiads* may never actually have visited Macau, but don't try telling the local Portuguese. Luis Vaz de Camões specialized in overblown,

Macau's History

The peninsula of Macau was first settled by the Portuguese in 1557 as a trading base and centre for Christianity. It was nearly taken by the Dutch in 1622, and struggled to survive through the next 250 years. The Portuguese tried to re-establish power in the mid-19th century, and managed to annexe the neighbouring islands of Taipa and Coloane. It could never compete with Hong Kong, however, and gambling, opium and prostitution continued to be the main draws. With the waning of colonial power, the Portuguese eventually gave the enclave back to China in December 1999.

patriotic verse – a bust of him peers through the grotto's gloom. The adjoining gardens ar popular with old men and their caged birds first thing in the morning. ✎ *6am–9pm • Free*

8 Forteleza do Monte

These walls bounded the original Portuguese settlement

Forteleza do Monte

Colonial-style buildings

Macau, a well-stocked fort, which its inhabitants boasted could withstand years of siege. The sternest test came in 1622 when the Dutch, who had been coveting Macau for years, made their move, only to be decisively beaten. The Portuguese military were based here up until 1966, at which point Portugal decided it was more politic to be administrators of Macau rather than gun-toting colonialists. ◕ *6am–7pm daily • Free*

9 Dom Pedro Theatre

The first Western-style lyric theatre in the East, the Dom Pedro opened in 1858. Recent renovations have seen it again hosting plays and performances after years of neglect. The hike up the hill is worth it for a look at a piece of theatrical history. ◕ *9am–6pm • Macau Tourism Office for performance details • 315 5666*

10 St Joseph's Seminary

The Jesuits constructed this ornate lemon-yellow chapel between 1746 and 1758, modelled on the Bon Gesu Basilica in Rome. Its original dedication plaque, recently unearthed, namechecks Portuguese King João V, Macau Bishop Hilario de St Rosa and Chinese Qing-dynasty Emperor Kien Lum. The 200-year-old bells still ring out each day, and all sorts of fascinating Catholic artifacts can be found within.

A Day in Macau

Morning

🕐 Catch a taxi to the **Ruinas de São Paulo** *(see p119)* in the heart of Macau, pose for a picture on the steps in front, then lose yourself in the surrounding streets full of Chinese and antique furniture shops. The rich red lacquered trunks and cabinets, old teak tables and chairs are all cheaper than in Hong Kong's antique stores.

When your feet start to protest, take a cab across the causeways to Coloane Island and a sangria-soaked lunch at **Fernando's** *(see p125)*. Get a large jug of piquant Sangria in, then go for the fried chicken, garlic prawns, clams and sardines. The bread is hot and moreish, and the Portuguese salad is simplistic bliss.

After Lunch

Walk off lunch on **Hac Sa Beach** *(see p122)* or wobble your way to the minibus outside Fernando's and travel to Taipa village, which has picturesque houses and shops.

It's easiest to hail a cab to get back to Macau. Stop off at the **Hotel Lisboa** *(see p123)* to ponder the flagship casino's seedy ambience. If you fancy a flutter, go ahead, but bear in mind that most of its customers are confirmed gambling junkies.

If you manage a win or can stop while you still have cash, head for Avenida Dr Sun Yat-Sen and its myriad bars for a night on the tiles. Maybe start at **Moonwalker**, then pop upstairs to **Signal** *(see p124)*.

Left **Lou Lim Ieoc Garden** Centre **Rua da Felicidade** Right **Maritime Museum**

Best of the Rest

1 Macau Tower
Locals have dubbed it "Dr Ho's erection" in honour of casino mogul Dr Stanley Ho. At 338 m (1,107 ft), it pips Paris's Eiffel Tower and is the centrepiece of a planned theme park and restaurant complex. The glass floor revolving restaurant is not for the faint of heart. ◈ *Nam Van Lakes area*

2 Pousada de Coloane
Macau's first beachfront hotel is a top spot for a few cold drinks when the sun is shining. ◈ *Cheoc Van Beach, Coloane • 882 143*

3 Lou Lim Ieoc Garden
Shady trees, lots of benches; lotus ponds. ◈ *Avenida do Conselheiro Ferreira De Almeida • 6am–6pm daily*

4 Macau Museum
Good displays on history and architecture. ◈ *Citadel of Sao Paolo do Monte • 357 911 • 10am– 6pm. Closed Mon • Adm*

5 Sao Domingos
The pale yellow Spanish-style church towers over the Largo do Senado square. White ants forced extensive renovations in the mid-1990s. More than 300 sacred works of art are in the adjoining museum. ◈ *Largo do Domingos • 10am–6pm daily • Free*

6 Sun Yat Sen Memorial House
The so-called "father of modern China" once resided in Macau, and his first wife continued to live here after he left. ◈ *Avenida Sidonio Pais • 10am–5pm, 2:30pm–5pm. Closed Tue • Free*

7 Rua da Felicidade
The "street of happiness" once teemed with brothels, hence its somewhat ironically bestowed name. It's now a quaint, cobbled thoroughfare full of cheap eateries.

8 Maritime Museum
The place to head if you are interested in Macau's colourful seagoing past. ◈ *Rua de Sao Tiago da Barra • 595 481 • 10am–5:30pm. Closed Tue • Adm*

9 Pousada de Sao Tiago
The beautiful hotel *(see p154)* overlooking the bay began life in the 17th century as a Portuguese fort hewn from the rock. ◈ *Avenida da Republica • 378 111*

10 Hac Sa Beach
Black mineral sand beach. Enjoy a stroll around the headland to the Westin Resort *(see p154)* for a drink. ◈ *Coloane*

Left **Hotel Lisboa** Centre **Floating Casino** Right **Kam Pek Casino**

10 Places to Gamble

1 Hotel Lisboa
Casino mogul Dr Stanley Ho's flagship looks like a UFO crossed with a wedding cake, and remains one of Macau's most bizarre landmarks. Expect loan sharks and grim-faced gamblers in rumpled clothes. ◈ 2–4 Avenida de Lisboa • 377 666 • Open 24 hours

2 Macau Jockey Club
A bit more down-at-heel than its high-tech, cashed-up Hong Kong counterpart. ◈ Eststrada Gov Albano da Oliveira, Taipa • 821 188 • Race meetings Wed or Thu & weekends • Adm

3 Canidrome
Go the dishlickers! This is the only greyhound racing club in Asia. ◈ Avenida General Castelo Branco • 221 199 • Tue, Thu & weekends • Adm

4 Floating Casino
An old converted ferry lit up like a Christmas tree. Crowded, ill-ventilated, smoky – everything a casino should be. ◈ Western waterfront, near the Hong Kong-Macau Jetfoil Terminal • 24 hours

5 Mandarin Oriental Casino
The more genteel side of gambling. Well-dressed, urbane punters sip martinis. ◈ Avenida da Amizade • 567 888 • 24 hours

6 Jai Alai Casino
Named after the world's fastest ball game, played in Cuba and Mexico. They used to play it in Macau, too, tossing the hard ball around at lethal speeds with curved wicker baskets, but it died out in the 1980s. ◈ Opp Jetfoil Terminal • 24 hours

7 Diamond Casino
Tucked away on the first floor of the Holiday Inn, the smallish Diamond casino has a relatively classy crowd. ◈ Rua De Pequim • 24 hours

8 Kingsway Hotel Casino
One of Macau's newest casinos, it rates high on the glitz scale. Minimum bets are higher here than in other casinos, so it's not for novices. ◈ Rua de Luis Gonagaza Gomes • 24 hours

9 Kam Pek Casino
Has a loyal clientele of local punters who can be downright rude to tourists and flashy Hong Kongers. Prolonged eye contact with habitués inadvisable. ◈ Opp Floating Casino • 24 hours

10 Hyatt Regency Hotel Casino
On Taipa Island so less intense than its Macau counterparts. ◈ 2 Estrada Almirante Marques Esperteiro • 831 234 • 24 hours

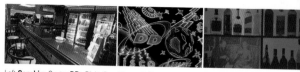

Left **Sanshiro** Centre **DDs** Right **Casablanca Café**

Cafés, Bars and Clubs

1 Signal Café

Best of the pack on the new Dynasty Plaza waterfront reclamation area. Stark and stylish décor, fairyland harbour views and a mix of local and Hong Kong DJs playing commercial and underground sounds. ◈ *1/F Vista Magnifica Court, Avenida Dr Sun Yat-Sen • $*

2 Opiarium Café

Cosy couches, great views, live bands. Only problem is, it closed its doors recently due to licensing problems and its reopening date remains up in the air. Check first if it's back in business. ◈ *Avenida Dr Sun Yat Sen • $*

3 Sanshiro

Kicks off late, after 10pm, as does most of Macau's nightlife. Good mix of sounds, cool vibe. ◈ *Avenida Dr Sun Yat Sen*

4 Macau Jazz Club

Bigger but not so atmospheric as the smoky, back-street hole-in-the-wall it replaced. Nearby, the tall gold Goddess of Mercy statue smiles sadly down at groovers with incipient hangovers. Live music after 9pm. ◈ *Avenida Dr Sun Yat Sen*

5 Oskar's Pub

Typical hotel-style pub with a mix of tourists, locals and the odd exponent of the world's oldest profession. ◈ *G/F Holiday Inn Hotel, Rua de Pequim*

6 Embassy Bar

Interesting mix of colonial artifacts, not to mention the antique racing car. ◈ *G/F Mandarin Oriental Hotel, Avenida da Amidaze*

7 Talker Pub

Fiesty locals at play, so tread carefully. There's always football on the television and cheap beer. ◈ *104 Rua de Pedro Coutinho*

8 DDs

Huge new club abounding with all manner of nocturnal creatures, including the odd triad *(see p90)*. ◈ *Underground complex opp Sintra Hotel, Avenida Dom Joao V*

9 Moonwalker

You won't see "moonwalker" Michael Jackson, but the harbour view from this popular bar is magical. ◈ *Vista Magnifica Court, Avenida Marginal da Baia*

10 Casablanca Café

There's a pool table, lots of red velvet and posters recalling the famous film. Resist the temptation to say "play it again, Sam" to the surly bar staff. ◈ *Avenida Dr Carlos Assumpcao, Dynasty Plaza*

Left **Grilled sardines, Fernando's** Right **Clube Militar de Macau**

Places to Eat

1 Fernando's

Still unspoiled by its far-flung fame, Fernando's is the perfect place for a long, lazy liquid lunch. Succulent roast chicken, grilled sardines, killer sangria and garlic prawns to die for. ◈ *9 Hac Sa Beach, Coloane • 882 531 (booking rec) • No credit cards • $$*

2 A Lorcha

A fine proponent of Macanese cooking, which blends the cuisines of East and West. Try spicy grilled African chicken, *bacalhau* (baked codfish) and *caldo verde* (potato purée soup). ◈ *289 Rua do Almirante Sergio • 313 193 • $*

3 Barra Nova

Next door to A Lorcha, and a reasonable alternative. More good, hearty Portuguese and Macanese cooking. ◈ *287A Rua do Almirante Sergio • 965 118 • $$*

4 Solmar

An old favourite among locals. Try the rich seafood soup with chunks of codfish that melt in your mouth. ◈ *512 Avenida da Praia Grande • 574 391 • $$*

5 Bolo de Arroz

Portuguese residents who stayed on after Handover come here for coffee and cakes. ◈ *11 Travesa de Sao Domingos • 339 089 • No credit cards • $*

6 Mezzaluna

Flickering half-moon candles reflect this romantic Italian restaurant's name. Best pasta in Macau and a fine selection of wines. ◈ *Mandarin Oriental Hotel, 956-1110 Avenida de Amizade • 567 888 • $$$*

7 Clube Militar de Macau

Built to cater for army bigwigs, the Military Club is one of the finest examples of classical European architecture in Asia. Gourmet Portuguese cuisine. ◈ *975 Avenida da Praia Grande • 714 010 • $$$*

8 Flamingo

Ducks paddle in the pond amid lush greenery as you soak up the atmosphere on the terrace. The food is European with a touch of Asia. ◈ *6/F Hyatt Regency, 2 Estrada Almirante Marques Esperteiro • 831 234 • $$$*

9 O Manel

Chef Manel is a local legend for his *bacalhau*. He imports prime Norwegian cod, salted in Portugal and grilled. ◈ *90 Rua Fernao Mendes Pinto, Taipa Village • 827 571 • $$*

10 Cozinha Pinocchio

Try the Portuguese spicy prawns, roast pigeon and curried crab at this institution. ◈ *4 Rua do Sol, Taipa Village • 827 128 • $$*

Note: Unless otherwise stated, all restaurants accept credit cards

Left **Crabs, Dong Men food market** Left **Minsk World** Right **Splendid China theme park**

Shenzhen

WITHIN LIVING MEMORY, Shenzhen, just across the New Territories border, was a minor township in communist China, its communal fisheries set in extraordinary juxtaposition to capitalist Hong Kong. Yet Shenzhen (or "Shumchun") has gone from gulag to Gotham City in the space of 20 years. The reason is its status as a free-trading Special Economic Zone, which has created wealth and allured schemers, tricksters and beggars from all over China. To them, Shenzhen is an ersatz Hong Kong; to the visitor, Shenzhen's tawdry commercialism offers a glimpse of the brave new China. Enjoyable, assuming you maintain a stiff sense of irony.

🔟 Sights

1. Lo Wu Commercial City
2. Dong Men District
3. Minsk World
4. Window of the World
5. Splendid China
6. China Folk Culture Village
7. Happy Valley
8. Mission Hills Golf Club
9. Bargain Beauty Treatments
10. Honey Lake Resort

Lo Wu Commercial City

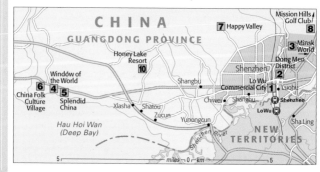

1 Lo Wu Commercial City

Right by the border station, this mall is the best and most convenient place to shop in Shenzhen. Inside its teeming five stories are virtually all the consumer goods you could ever desire,

Minsk World

in exhaustive and exhausting quantities. The brands are either Chinese (often of solid build) or fake Western (take your chances). Countless stalls sell all manner of clothes, footwear, jewellery, watches, accessories and electronic goods. A huge textiles market is on the fifth floor. For real bargains try to haggle down to half the original asking price. ◈ *By border stn*

2 Dong Men District

If you have the energy to tackle it, a vast expanse of clothes shops awaits you in the sprawling Dong Men district. Remember that clothes such as men's shirts will be cut for the Asian figure, meaning cuffs coming up to your elbows, so try before buying. At the eastern edge of Dong Men is a footbridge leading to another huge fabric market, located above a food market. There is no English signposting here, though, so be sure to have the destination written down in Chinese. ◈ *Dong Men district, a couple of miles N of Lowu*

3 Minsk World

The ironies come thick and fast aboard this former Soviet aircraft carrier, selling American hot dogs from its flight deck. It's a hugely popular destination for Chinese tourists, though few Westerners visit. Here you can thrill at footage of missiles exploding in fireballs of increasing magnitude set against a spaghetti western soundtrack; behold stuffed Russian space dog Strelka; and applaud a baffling Russian cabaret act. ◈ *Yantian district • 755 535 5333 • 9:30am–4pm daily • Adm*

4 Window of the World

Of all the oddities springing from Shenzhen's fevered theme parks appetite, Window of the World is, to Western eyes, the most surreal: a reduction (literally and metaphorically) of the real world. Mount Fuji becomes a 6-m (20-ft) slagheap, tourists pose in Thai national dress in front of the Taj Mahal and, poignantly, Manhattan retains its World Trade Center. Live shows are put on at set times on most "continents", including one from a suspiciously Asiatic-looking African tribe. There's also a Grand Canyon flume ride and a real snow ski-slope. ◈ *Overseas Chinese Town • 86 755 660 8000 • 9am– 9pm weekdays, 9am–10:30pm weekends • Adm*

Window of the World

Minsk World *(sidebar)*

For mainland China visa information **See p136**

Left and Right **Splendid China**

Splendid China
5 The architectural wonders of China, including recreations of Beijing's Imperial Palace, the Terracotta Warriors of Xian and the Great Wall. ✎ *Overseas Chinese Town • 755 660 0626 • 10am–10:30pm weekdays, 10am–8pm weekends • Adm*

China Folk Culture Village
6 Full-size recreations of traditional villages are peopled by well groomed, eternally happy folk representing different ethnic Chinese groups. An anthropologist's nightmare perhaps, but it will give you some idea of China's diverse cultural and ethnic melting pot. ✎ *Overseas Chinese Town • 755 660 0626 • 10am–10:30pm weekdays, 10am–8pm weekends • Adm*

Happy Valley
7 This theme park gives Hong Kong's Ocean Park a run for its money, with the bonus of a tidal pool, adrenalin-inducing rides such as the Space Shot, an assault course and martial arts demonstrations. Use the Happy Line monorail to travel between this and other nearby theme parks ✎ *Overseas Chinese Town • 755 569 49168 • 9:30am–9pm daily • Adm*

Mission Hills Golf Club
8 Many Hong Kong executives come across the border to play at this five-star, 90-hole golf club. Alternatively, you can play tennis on one of the resort's 51 courts. ✎ *Mission Hills Rd, Guanlan town • Reservations 2973 0303*

Bargain Beauty Treatments
9 When you reach breaking point with all the shopping malls and theme parks, rest and refresh yourself with an exceptionally cheap foot or back massage, or perhaps some nail painting. A vast range of treatments are available at Lo Wu *(see p127).* Hotel health centres offer the assurance of professional reflexology and traditional massage. Submitting to several treatments at the same time is the last word in pampering.

Honey Lake Resort
10 Away from Shenzhen's urban stresses, almost every kind of leisure facility is on the doorstep at Honey Lake, including a large amusement park, shopping mall, golf courses and indoor and outdoor pools. ✎ *Shennan Rd, Futian district • 755 370 8988 • Adm*

Mission Hills Golf Club

Price Categories

For a three-course meal for one with half a bottle of wine (or equivalent meal) and extra charges.

$	under HK$100
$$	HK$100–250
$$$	HK$250–450
$$$$	HK$450–600
$$$$$	Over HK$600

Laurel Restaurant

🔟 Places to Eat and Drink

1 Laurel Restaurant
Terrific classic Cantonese restaurant that is packed all day but worth a wait. 🔊 Shop 5010, 5/F, Lo Wu Commercial City • 232 3668 • $$

2 Nishimura
Low-key eatery, one of only a few Japanese food places in Shenzhen. Reasonably priced sushi, sashimi, teppanyaki and shobotayaki. 🔊 2/F, Shangri-La Hotel, Jianshe Rd • 233 0888 • No credit cards • $$

3 Luohu
Inside its ornate pagoda-style exterior you'll find familiar Cantonese fare including seafood fresh from the fishtanks and dim sum. Busy, popular and slightly cheaper than Hong Kong prices. 🔊 Jianshe Road, 1/F Luohu Bldg • No credit cards • 225 2827 • $$$

4 Tiara
With great night views of Shenzhen, the revolving restaurant atop the luxury Shangri-La Hotel (see p148) has an international buffet, hotpots and grills. 🔊 Shangri-La Hotel, Jianshe Rd • 233 0888 x8230 • $$$$

5 Yen Yen
Not much to look at, but the greasy-spoon style Yen Yen has a great Cantonese menu. 🔊 G/F, Jin Cheng Bldg, Shennan Dong Lu, Lo Wu • 223 4168 • No credit cards • $

6 Henry J Beans
When you simply have to have that burger, head to Henry J Beans. It also has one of Shenzhen's few decent bars without Vegas-style glitter or deafening Karaoke. 🔊 2/F, Shangri-La Hotel, Jianshe Road • 233 0888 • $$

7 BB's Bar and Brewery Restaurant
The all-you-can-eat Brazilian buffet at the Landmark caters to dedicated carnivores, serving carved meat like it's going out of fashion. The home-made beer is cheap too. 🔊 The Landmark, 3018 Nanhu Rd • 217 2288 • $$

8 Casablanca
French-influenced international food in Shekou district, which is Shenzhen's ex-pat, harbourside bolthole. 🔊 G/F, Yin Bin Building, Taizi Lu, Shekou • 667 5922 • No credit cards • $$

9 Halftooth
Another Shekou option, serving Thai food, with evening barbecues at weekends. 🔊 12 Bi Hua Lu, Crystal Garden, Shekou • 329 3278 • No credit cards • $$

Nishimura Restaurant

10 Piazza Café
For a sumptuous, excellent-value, seafood dinner head to the Landmark's coffee shop, and look for the buffet. 🔊 1/F, The Landmark, 2 Nanhu Rd • 217 2288 • $$

Unless otherwise stated, all restaurants accept credit cards

Left **Street scene** Centre **Martial arts in the park** Right **White Swan Hotel, Shamian Island**

Guangzhou

CHINA'S TWO GREAT REVOLUTIONS, republican and communist, were born in Guangzhou (or what the West used to call "Canton"), which indicate the temperament of this sprawling southern Chinese capital. Far distant from Beijing, the city has gone its own wilful way, and there is still the insouciance and restlessness of a people who answer to no-one. The modern city is at the mercy of miasmic smog and yammering traffic, but it also has enormous personality, from Han dynasty tombs to a rich choice of temples, traditional architecture and the charm of Shamian Island's faded 19th-century terraces.

🔟 Sights in Guangzhou

1. Shamian Island
2. Wandering Among the Gei
3. Hua Lin Temple and Jade Market
4. Chen Clan Temple
5. Temples of Filial Piety and Six Banyan Trees
6. Nanyue Tomb
7. Yuexiu Park
8. White Cloud Mountain
9. Guangdong Museum of Art
10. River Trips

Pagoda at Six Banyan Trees

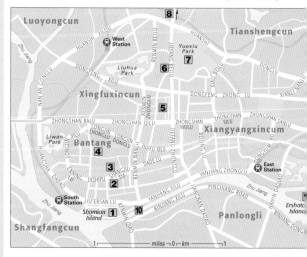

Left **Wandering among the** *gei* Left **Chen Clan Temple**

1 Shamian Island

The small islet in southwest Guangzhou long served as the main gateway to China, the only place where merchants and diplomats were allowed to do business with the Empire. Today it's a lovely leafy haven, recently restored and beautified with some good accommodation, dining and drinking options and quiet riverside walks.

2 Wandering Among the Gei

Perhaps the simplest yet most worthwhile thing to do in Guangzhou is to wander aimlessly along its *geis*, the narrow alleys between the ancient ramshackle houses in the older parts of town. The streets above Shamian Island up as far as Liwanhu district are especially good. Strolling down these byways gives a sense of the everyday life that has carried on here for hundreds of years. Absorb yourself in the minutiae of domestic life and small-scale

Jade market

industries, such as beauty treatments, maybe in the form of eyebrow plucking with a simple piece of cotton.

3 Hua Lin Temple and Jade Market

An extensive jade market surrounds the small Buddhist temple of Hua Lin, which is also worth a quick visit. The jade on sale is cheaper than in Hong Kong, although you'll need to be an expert if you want good-quality, unpigmented examples. Several antique stores and jade and amber sellers can be found west of Kangwang Zhonglu, and north of Changshang Xilu. ◈ *North of Xiaju Lu, east of Wenc Nan Wenlu*

4 Chen Clan Temple

With Chen being the most common family name in the area, it's no surprise that the many groupings of local Chens constructed a suitably vast temple complex in the 1890s. It's particularly worth a look if you haven't visited any of the ancestral halls in the New Territories of Hong Kong. The most impressive feature is the ornate ceramic friezes adorning the roof, which depict legendary beasts. There are also displays (some of admittedly patchy quality) of jade, bone and other local crafts, some for sale. Head to the leafy courtyards for peace and shade. ◈ *On way to Foshan* • *8:30am–5:30pm daily* • *Adm*

For mainland China visa information **See p136**

Left **Temple of the Six Banyan Trees** Right **Yuexiu Park**

Temples of Filial Piety and Six Banyan Trees

The Temple of Filial Piety (Guangxiao Si) was a royal temple as far back as the 2nd century BC, and is thought to have served as a Buddhist shrine since the 4th century AD. However, the buildings that stand today were built in the 17th century. It's a lovely place to come and sit beneath venerable, ancient fig trees in quiet courtyards. The nearby Temple of the Six Banyan Trees (Liurong Si) has the oldest and largest pagoda in Guangzhou, standing at 55 m (180 ft), though the banyan trees have sadly died. ◈ On Hongshu Lu, just off Zhongshan Lu

Nanyue Tomb

A well-presented museum preserves the burial tomb and artifacts of one of the kings of the Southern Yue, who ruled the area in the 2nd and 3rd centuries AD. Well signposted in Chinese and English, the tomb offers a glimpse of a culturally sophisticated society. Fine ceramic pillows and exquisite packaging materials from later dynasties are among the displays. ◈ Jeifang Beilu • 9am–5pm daily • Adm

Yuexiu Park

The lovely expanse of park contains a sculpture of the Five Rams, the symbol of Guangzhou, and a monument to Sun Yat-Sen, the revered former Hong Kong resident and grandfather of the Chinese revolution. The Municipal Museum is housed in the Zhen Hai Tower, the last remnant of the city's 14th-century walls. ◈ Park 7am–7pm • Adm • Museum 9am–5pm daily • Adm

White Cloud Mountain

Overlooking the city haze is a huge wooded area dominated by a series of ridges and peaks, offering open space, fresh air and cooling breezes.

Guangdong Museum of Art

Probably still China's largest art museum, displaying ancient and contemporary Chinese art. ◈ Ersha Island • 9am–5pm Tue–Sun • Adm

River Trips

Escape the fumes and look back on the city from the river. A number of operators offer cruises. Try an evening trip on the *White Swan*, a lovely old masted yacht.

Five Rams sculpture, Yeuxiu Park

Unless otherwise stated, all restaurants accept credit cards

Lucy's Restaurant

Price Categories

For a three-course meal for one with half a bottle of wine (or equivalent meal) and extra charges.

$	under HK$100
$$	HK$100–250
$$$	HK$250–450
$$$$	HK$450–600
$$$$$	Over HK$600

🔟 Places to Eat and Drink

1 J M Chef (aka Kiu Mei)
Those of a nervous disposition may want to skip the "frog milk" and "stewed insect in pot", but the sizzling "chicken with three cups wine" is terrific. ◈ Opp White Swan Hotel, Shamian Island • 8191 3018 • No credit cards • $$

2 Lucy's
The chilled-out atmosphere makes it a good place to wind down, though the Western and Chinese food isn't prize-winning, and the drinks are relatively expensive. ◈ 3 Shamian St South, Shamian Island • 8187 4106 • No credit cards • $$

J M Chef

3 Banana Leaf
Good, cheap Thai and South-east Asian food in this bright and popular venue. Try the juices and teas with fruit and honey. ◈ 1/F Broadcasting and Television Hotel, 8 Lu Ju Lu • 8359 1288 x3118 • $$

4 Windflower Pub
Currently Guangzhou's coolest bar, this is where the beautiful people flock. ◈ 387 Huanshi Donglu

5 Hill Bar
Not for seekers of fine dining, but the slightly seedy ambience, central location and late hours make this a great beer and munchies stop. ◈ 367 Huanshi Donglu • 8333 3998 • No credit cards • $

6 Champs Elysees
After hauling yourself up four flights of stairs to reach the door, expect to pay over the odds for the theming here. That said, the French, Italian and Mediterranean food is good. Try the extensive couscous menu. ◈ Huanshi Donglu • 8385 6230 • $$

7 My Home Restaurant
Something of a local institution for very spicy Hunanese dishes. ◈ 19 Tao Jin Lu • 8559 2101 • No credit cards • $

8 Bai Yun Yi Feng Restaurant
Worth a stop if you're visiting White Cloud Mountain and fancy dim sum or congee (rice porridge). ◈ Nr cable car terminus • 8770 6871-2322 • No credit cards • $

9 White Swan Coffee Shop
Best for its all-you-can-eat international lunch buffet with good sushi and seafood. ◈ White Swan Hotel, 1 Southern St, Shamian Island • 8188 6968 • $$

🔟 Xiang Cun Guan
Smart, minimalist and serving unpretentious Hunanese cuisine (consider the spicy hotpots). Have someone write the name in Chinese and take a cab, or spend all day trying to find it. ◈ 23 Xian Lie Nanlu • 8778 9888 x86128 • No credit cards • $$

Following pages **Gardeners in central Hong Kong**

STREETSMART

STREETSMART

Left **Hong Kong Airport** Centre **British brand shop** Right **Road signs in Chinese and English**

TOP 10 Planning Your Trip

1 Passport and Visa Information

Citizens from the UK, US, Canada, Australia and New Zealand need only a valid passport to enter Hong Kong. UK citizens may stay up to six months and US, Canadian, Australian and New Zealand visitors for up to three months without a visa. (Ensure your passport is valid for at least a month after you plan to leave Hong Kong.) To visit mainland China (beyond the New Territories), you will need a visa. These are easy to obtain when you are in Hong Kong, from travel agents. China Travel Service issues China visas for HK\$150 (or HK\$300 to process in 24 hours). You'll need to leave your passport and one passport photo. Citizens of most countries may visit Macau for up to 20 days without a visa – Portuguese citizens are allowed 90 days.

2 When to Go

The milder months from October to late January are a popular time to visit, although Hong Kong's climate is at its best in March and April. Hotel rooms will be heavily booked and more expensive in October and April. Flights also tend to be heavily booked during these months.

3 Climate

Just south of the Tropic of Cancer, Hong Kong's sub-tropical climate has a mild winter (December–February) when temperatures can drop as low as 10°C (50°F), while spring (March–April) and autumn (October–November) are short, warm and pleasant. In summer (May–September), temperatures average about 28°C (83°F), relative summer humidity regularly soars above 80 or 90 per cent and typhoons and tropical storms often visit.

4 What to Take

Light clothing will suffice for most of the year. A long-sleeved top is advisable for some of the arctic air-conditioning; a light jacket for the winter months.

5 Languages

Cantonese, Mandarin and English are the official languages of Hong Kong. English is widely understood and spoken, so English-speakers will find it easy to get around, although expect communication difficulties with taxi drivers and residents in remoter rural areas.

6 Health Preparations

No compulsory vaccinations are required for Hong Kong, but a yellow fever vaccination is necessary if you are visiting southern China from a yellow fever infected area. Common medical and hygiene products are readily available. Ensure you have valid medical insurance.

7 Currency Information

The local currency is the Hong Kong dollar (HK\$) divided into 100 cents. Bills are issued in 20-, 50-, 100-, 500- and 1,000-dollar denominations. Coins come in 1-, 2-, 5- and 10-dollar and 10-, 20- and 50-cent denominations. Pegged to the US dollar, the exchange rate always hovers close to HK\$7.8 to the US\$1.

8 Money

Take lots! Hong Kong can be expensive. There is no limit on the amount that can be changed *(see also p142)*.

9 Local Prices

Hong Kong is not the shopper's paradise it once was. Many branded and designer goods are on par with or even pricier than in the West. Bargains can be found, however, in the markets *(see pp38–9)* and warehouse outlets *(see pp76 & 101)*.

10 Driving Licences

A valid international driving licence is required for driving and car hire.

Directory

China Travel Service
78–83 Connaught Rd, Central • 2853 3888

Left **Airport train** Centre **Macau Airport** Right **Passenger ferry**

10 Getting to Hong Kong

1 Direct Flights
Being a major hub, Hong Kong is well served by direct connections to much of the globe. Major cities linked by direct flights to Hong Kong include: Auckland, Sydney, Melbourne, LA, London, San Francisco, Toronto and Vancouver.

2 Stopovers
There are plenty of stopover options for breaking your journey. Singapore, Kuala Lumpur and Bangkok can make interesting and cheap stopover breaks if flying in from the west, or Seoul and Taipei if flying in from the east. Most carriers do not charge for arranging inbound and outbound stopovers; some even offer special deals.

3 Booking Flights and Hotels Online
Flight and hotel deals are worth checking on the websites listed in the directory. Note some reserve bookings from the US or UK only.

4 Finding the Cheapest Flights
The cheapest times to head to Hong Kong are just after Chinese New Year in early January, and from November to mid-December. Late deals can sometimes be found on websites such as lastminute.co.uk. Booking well in advance can also secure lower prices.

Some websites, such as travelocity.com, offer e-mail services alerting you when tickets fall below a certain price. Bargains are less likely if your return leg falls in August, or between Christmas and Chinese New Year, when many locals fly out.

5 Flights from Southeast Asia
If you'll be spending time in Southeast Asia first, very competitively priced air tickets to Hong Kong can be bought from the Asian hubs of Bangkok, Kuala Lumpur and Singapore.

6 Information at the Airport
There are tourist information offices in transfer area T2 and the arrivals buffer halls A and B. There's also a hotel information and reservations office in the arrivals halls.

7 Cross-Country Route by Rail
For those with time and money, the most adventurous way to reach Hong Kong from Europe is by rail via the Trans-Siberia Railway, through Mongolia or Manchuria to Beijing, and then connecting to Hong Kong. For background, see www.trailblazer-guides.com and *The Trans-Siberian Handbook* by Bryn Thomas.

8 Rail Routes from China
Hong Kong-bound trains depart regularly each day from Guangzhou. Sleeper services between Beijing and Shanghai depart on alternate days. "Soft" sleeper compartments are plush and less crowded but can cost almost as much as flying.

9 By Sea
Fast, regular ferry services to Hong Kong run from Guangzhou and Macau. Services from Macau take anywhere between one and two hours and from Guangzhou two to three hours.

10 By Road
Several buses also run daily between Guangzhou and Hong Kong.

Directory

Websites
www.expedia.com
www.priceline.com
www.priceline.co.uk
www.travelocity.com
www.cheaptickets.com
www.bargainflights.com
www.lastminute.co.uk
www.trailblazer-guides.com
www.cathaypacific.com

Airport Information
General information booths 2807 6543, 7am–11pm daily
• *www.hkairport.com*
• *Hotel reservation desks 6am–1pm daily*

Left **MTR logo** Centre **Taxi** Right **Tram**

🔟 Getting Around Hong Kong

1 Airport Transfer Options

The excellent, modern airport trains to Central take just 23 minutes and depart every 10 minutes from 6am to 1:30am daily. Taxis are also readily available at the airport. The E11 bus through Central, Wanchai and Causeway Bay takes about an hour and is the cheapest option.

2 Octopus Cards

If you're going to travel widely in Hong Kong consider buying an Octopus card, which you charge with money and swipe over the readers on most local buses, trains, ferries and trams. You can buy and charge cards at the airport or KCR train stations.

3 The MTR and KCR

The excellent, efficient MTR (Mass Transit Railway) system runs from 6am to 1.30am on five underground lines connecting Hong Kong Island, Kowloon, the New Territories and Lantau. It's clean, cheap and air-conditioned. The KCR (Kowloon-Canton Railway) line, connecting Kowloon with the New Territories, runs from 5.30am to 1am.

4 Buses

Cheap, frequent buses connect almost every place in Hong Kong. Pick up a bus route map at any of the HKTA's offices. Major hotels offer free shuttle buses between the hotels and Kowloon and Central KCR stations.

5 Taxis

Red taxis operate in and around central Hong Kong and are reasonably priced. Surcharges apply for tunnel tolls, luggage in the trunk and late-night journeys. Tipping is appreciated but not expected. Green taxis run in the New Territories; blue ones on Lantau. Bear in mind, though, that few taxi drivers can speak much English.

6 Ferries

Ferries link Hong Kong Island with Kowloon, the outlying islands, Macau and China. The frequent Star Ferries *(see pp14–15)* shuttle between Hong Kong and Tsim Sha Tsui on Kowloon from 6:30am to 11:30pm. Next to Central's Star Ferry pier are the main piers for outlying islands.

7 Trams

The ancient, wood-panelled, double-deck trams running west to east from Kennedy Town to Chai Wan are a slow, sometimes cramped but undeniably atmospheric way to get around Hong Kong. A very reasonable flat fee applies for all destinations. The legendary Peak Tram *(see p9)* leaves from Garden Road.

8 By Foot

The best way to see many central Hong Kong districts is to walk. The distances are short, although the inclines can be steep. Walking is really the only way to see the sights in Western, the Mid-Levels, Wan Chai, much of Kowloon and Hong Kong's country parks. Walking in parts of Central and Admiralty, however, can be a disorientating trudge around a maze of walkways and underpasses.

9 By Bike

Forget cycling amon the urban congestion an fumes, but think about hiring a bike to hit some of the rugged, steep country trails. Contact the Hong Kong Cycling Association for details.

10 Car Hire and Driving

Why hire a car in Hong Kong when it's so easy to get around, parking is scarce and congestion i so intense? If you do, you'll need an international driving licence.

Directory

Hong Kong Cycling Association
2504 8176

Car Hire
Avis 2890 6988 • Hertz 2525 2838 • Trinity 2563 6117

Left Octopus travel cards Centre **Tourist information sign** Right **HKTB desk**

10 Sources of Information

1 HKTB Services
The Hong Kong Tourism Board (HKTB) has conveniently located branches offering brochures and advice. There is also a website and multi-lingual visitor hotline.

2 Websites
HKTB's website *(see Directory)* is a good starting point. Others include the *South China Morning Post's* www.scmp.com and www.totallyhk.com. For directory services go to www.hkt.com.

3 Newspapers
The broadsheet daily *South China Morning Post* provides extensive coverage of local, Chinese and world news. The tabloid *i-mail* offers less comprehensive coverage and an irreverent spin.

4 Local Magazines
HK Magazine (free) is a weekly listings magazine with eating, drinking and going out tips. *BC Magazine* (also free) is a clubbing-heavy, twice-monthly guide with listings. Both are available from bars and restaurants.

5 English-Language Radio and TV
ATV World and TVB Pearl are Hong Kong's two terrestrial English-language channels. RTHK is Hong Kong's publicly funded but editorially independent radio broadcaster. RTHK 3 (567 AM, 1584AM) has mainly news,

finance and current affairs; RTHK 4 (96.7–98.9FM) plays Western and Chinese classical music, RTHK 6 (675AM) broadcasts BBC World Service programming.

6 Practical Books and Maps
The HKTB has free maps of central Hong Kong and free booklets including *A Guide to Quality Merchants*, *Hong Kong Access Guide for Disabled Visitors* and *Exploring Hong Kong's Countryside*, available in several languages. Good maps (the *Countryside Series*) are available from Government Publications Centres.

7 Business Information
The Hong Kong Trade Development Council (www.tdc.org.hk) offers useful information.

8 Facts and Figures
The government website, www.info.gov.hk, with links to all its departments, is a good starting point for facts and figures. The CIA's online World Factbook offers raw statistics on Hong Kong and China at: www.cia.gov/cia/publications/factbook/index.html

9 Weather and Air Quality Info
Hong Kong Observatory's phoneline and website offer daily and three-day forecasts. The Weather Underground site, www.

underground.org.hk, and *South China Morning Post* at http://weather.scmp.com also have local weather and air pollution information.

10 Some Books for Background
Hong Kong: A Guide to Recent Architecture by Juanita Cheng and Andrew Yeoh is a useful pocket guide. *A History of Hong Kong* by Frank Welsh starts from the time of British rule. *Travellers' Tales Guides: Hong Kong* includes some excellent writing from Jan Morris, Bruce Chatwin and Charles Jennings.

Directory

HKTB Website
www.discoverhong kong.com

HKTB Branches
Airport buffer halls and Area A2 • Tsim Sha Tsui Star Ferry terminal, Kowloon 8am–6pm daily • G/F, the Center, 99 Queen's Rd, Central • 8am–6pm daily

HKTA Hotline
2508 1234

Government Publications Centres
G/F, 66 Queensway, 2537 1910 • 382 Nathan Rd, Kowloon, 2780 0981

HK Observatory
2926 8200 • www.weather.gov.hk

Left **Busy road in Central** Right **Topless bar signs** Right **Public bus**

TOP 10 Things to Avoid

1 Driving in Central Hong Kong and Kowloon
Traffic is often bumper to bumper, so walk or take another form of transport.

2 Hurrying in Central on a Sunday
Filipino and Indonesian domestic workers crowd Central's sidewalks and squares on a Sunday, so don't expect anything other than slow progress. Watching these low-paid workers enjoying their only day off makes for a contrast, or perhaps rebuke, to the bustle and conspicuous consumption usually on display.

3 The Peak on a Sunday
Long queues form for the Peak Tram and the whole Peak area is much busier at weekends and particularly on Sundays. Turn round and come back another day if it's cloudy, too, as you'll miss those spectacular views.

4 Eating or Drinking on the MTR
Hong Kongers may blithely litter their streets, countryside and harbour, but no-one eats or drinks on the spotless subway.

5 Hostess Bars of Wanchai or Tsim Sha Tsui
That is unless you want to pay steep surprise cover charges on top of your already expensive drinks. These may still be popular destinations for US sailors on shore leave, but don't expect to recapture the world of Suzy Wong.

6 Illegal Drug Use
Expect to be arrested if you are found in possession of illegal drugs of any kind. Hong Kong law officially makes no distinction between the types of drug found. Spot checks and raids are sometimes carried out in areas such as Lan Kwai Fong.

7 Unfamiliar Areas Late at Night
There's no doubt Hong Kong is a relatively safe city, but don't tempt fate by wandering through quiet streets and heavily built-up housing areas in the dead of night. Take a taxi instead.

8 Traffic-Choked Areas
On smoggy days you can see, smell and taste the pollution in places such as Causeway Bay and Central. When the pollution index heads above 100, escape the smog by taking a trip out to the countryside or the outlying islands.

9 Taking a Bus Without the Right Change
No change is offered on buses, so take the right money, use an Octopus Card (see p138) or be prepared to lose the change owed to you.

10 Leaving a Rucksack Unattended
Backpackers staying in such places as the Chungking Mansions (see p15) should take particular care with rucksacks. Theft by unscrupulous fellow travellers is a possibility.

Directory

General Emergencies
999

Crime Hotline
2527 7177

Hospital Authority Enquiry Service
2300 6555
• www.ha.org.hk

The Adventist Hospital
40 Stubbs Rd, Happy Valley, Hong Kong Island • 2574 6211

Caritas Medical Centre
111 Wing Hong St, Sham Shui Po • 2746 7911

Matilda Hospital
41 Mount Kellet Rd, The Peak, Hong Kong Island • 2849 0375

Queen Mary Hospital
102 Pok Fu Lam Rd, Hong Kong Island • 2855 3838

Lost/Stolen Credit Cards
Amex 2811 6122
• MasterCard 800 966 677 toll free • VISA 800 967 025

Left **Crowded street scene** Centre **Hiking, the Wilson trail** Right **Traditional pharmacy**

🔟 Health and Security Tips

1 Foreign-Language Hotlines

Important information and emergency hotlines are efficient and provide foreign-language speakers mainly English.

2 Drinking Water and Food Safety

Hong Kong's tap water is safe to drink. Wash fresh fruit and vegetables. Avoid locally caught seafood if your health is fragile, as high pollution levels and some diseases can lurk in local fish. Many local restaurants source fish from abroad.

3 Air Pollution Advice

Urban air quality is improving rapidly following the introduction of cleaner vehicle fuels. Even so, the air pollution index can still head above 100, at which point people with respiratory complaints are advised to stay indoors. Consult the SCMP's website http://weather.scmp.com for regular updates.

4 Seawater Pollution and Swimming Dangers

Sadly, Hong Kong has made slow progress in treating the sewage it empties into its own waters, let alone in tackling the pollution washing from China's rivers. There are good beaches (usually government managed) but seawater quality can vary markedly. Toxic algae blooms occasionally make swimming unsafe. It's best to swim on a lifeguard-staffed beach with shark net. On unmanaged beaches never swim at dawn, dusk, in murky waters or with open wounds.

5 Avoiding Security Risks

Crime and theft directed at tourists are rare in Hong Kong. To be completely safe, take common-sense precautions such as keeping a close hold on personal possessions, using a hotel safe if provided and not leaving valuable items or documents in your backpack.

6 Other Security Precautions

If you are planning to spend time in Hong Kong, registering your passport with your local consulate or embassy will make replacing a lost one easier. Extra travel insurance may be a good idea if you are travelling with expensive items.

7 Heat and Humidity Precautions

Hydration is important at all times, especially so in Hong Kong's stifling summer heat and humidity. Ensure you drink plenty of fluid. Cool, light, loose cotton clothing will be most comfortable. Wear a hat if you are outdoors for long periods or turn your umbrella into a sun parasol. If you're worried about the heat, avoid too much activity during the hottest part of the day. Head up Victoria Peak for cooler climes or to the coast for sea breezes.

8 What to Take if Hiking

Don't underestimate your ability to sweat and lose fluid in the heat. Take lots of water. Buy a good map, take a mobile phone if you have one and small change for local transport. Sensible clothing and footwear are a must for walking unpaved trails. Pocket tissues might come in handy for some of the public toilets in rustic areas. In winter, take a waterproof.

9 Hospitals with A&E

Caritas Medical Centre and Queen Mary Hospital are among those with 24-hour accident and emergency departments.

10 Doctors and Dentists

The Adventist Hospital and the Matilda Hospital are both private hospitals with bilingual (Cantonese/English) staff. Their outpatient departments include those for women and travellers, and there are also maternity and dental clinics. See the *Yellow Pages* for more foreign-language doctors and dentists in Hong Kong.

Left **Bank window** Centre left **ATM** Centre **Phone boxes** Right **Man on a mobile**

Banking and Communications

1 Banks, ATMs and Credit Cards

Banks and ATMs are numerous. Opening hours are 9am–4:30pm Mon–Fri and 9am–12:30pm Sat. Most ATMs operate 24 hours. Credit/debit cards are widely accepted.

2 Money Changing and Forwarding

Banks offer the best foreign exchange rates, although there are plenty of independent bureaux de change. Using your bank card at an ATM may be cheaper than changing money or using travellers' cheques. Money forwarding can be arranged through local banks, or try Western Union.

3 Post

The Hong Kong postal service is rapid and efficient. Local mail takes one to two days. Zone 1 air mail (all of Asia except Japan) takes three to five days. Zone 2 (the rest of the world) takes five to seven days. The General Post Office operates Hong Kong's post restante service.

4 Telephones

Local calls in Hong Kong are free. Many hotel lobbies and shops will make phones available free for local calls. Coin-operated public phone boxes cost HK$1 minimum. Some accept credit cards or have Internet services. Phone cards for calling abroad

are available from convenience stores, some vending machines, the Star Ferry piers and HKTB offices (see p139).

5 Calling Hong Kong

The international code for Hong Kong is 852.

6 Mobile Phones

Hong Kong's mobile networks are GSM-based. Dual-band mobile phones will work in Hong Kong if you have set the service up with your home provider. Pacific Century CyberWorks (PCCW) has outlets offering phone rentals by the week. WAP services are available, but not advanced.

7 Local Internet Access

Internet access is plentiful, convenient, cheap and often free (see p143). Much of Hong Kong uses speedy broadband connections, including the main hotels, most of which have installed dual telephone/modem connectors into rooms.

8 Hong Kong Central Library

Hundreds of magazines and newspapers from around the world are available to read free at the shiny new main library in Causeway Bay. Internet access here is plentiful, fast and free (bookings taken for one hour at a time). There's

also a good café with outdoor seating.

9 Faxing

Faxing from business centres or photocopying shops is simple, although not cheap. Your hotel may offer a cheaper service and will accept faxes on your behalf.

10 Business Facilities

Hong Kong is well supplied with business centres and services. See Hong Kong's Yellow Pages. Business cards can be printed on Man Wa Lane in Sheung Wan, off Des Voeux Road West. Have your details translated into Chinese on the back.

Directory

Collect Calls
10010

Directory Services
1081

General Post Office
2 Connaught Place, Hong Kong Island
• 2921 2222

HKT Phone Rental
2883 3938

Main Library
66 Causeway Bay Rd, Hong Kong Island
• 2921 0208

Western Union
Star Ferry 2316 2608

United Centre
95 Queensway, Hong Kong Island • 2528 5631

Left **Temple** Centre **Cheap food stall** Right **Tai Chi**

🔟 Hong Kong on a Budget

1 Eating Cheap

Food kiosks and inexpensive Chinese restaurants abound. Fast food chains are competitive in Hong Kong. Lunchtime, all-you-can-eat buffets are also fairly common, or head to the Indian restaurants upstairs in Chungking Mansions (see p87).

2 Cheap Nights Out

Most bars offer long happy hours or promotions before a certain time of evening. Drink is free for women on certain nights at numerous bars. On race nights, soak up the atmosphere and some cheap beer at Happy Valley horseracing track (see pp12–13).

3 Cheap Days Out

There are plenty of options for cheap days out. Walk Hong Kong's wilderness trails (see pp46–7), nose around the market at Stanley (see p16), or walk the Dragon's Back path to Shek O (see p74). It need only cost the return bus fare and the price of a cheap lunch, which you can sleep off on the beach.

4 Free Buildings, Museums and Galleries

For dizzying views atop some of the world's tallest buildings head to the free viewing galleries on the 47th floor of the Bank of China Building in Central (see p42) and the 46th floor of Wanchai's Central Plaza (see p43). Hong Kong's museums and galleries are incredibly cheap to visit, but all have a free day each week and some are free all week.

5 Free Parks and Gardens

Hong Kong Park (see p59), which includes the excellent walk-through Edward Youde Aviary, and the Zoological and Botanical Gardens (see p54) nearby are well worth a visit and are completely free.

6 Free Tai Chi Lessons

Learn the slow, graceful, health-promoting moves of the traditional Chinese martial art Tai Chi for free under the Tsim Sha Tsui clocktower early on Tuesday and Wednesday mornings (see also p33).

7 Temples

Hong Kong's many temples are free (although some change for the collection box is appreciated). Try the Man Mo Temple on Hollywood Road (see p61), the Tin Hau Temple off Nathan Road in Yau Ma Tei (see p89) or the Wong Tai Sin Temple in eastern Kowloon (see p95).

8 Free Calls and Internet Access

Local telephone calls are usually free. Some hotel lobbies have telephones for free local calls. Internet access is plentiful, fast and free at the Convention Centre's Business Centre and at the Causeway Bay Main Library.

9 Free Cultural Events

For free music head to the foyer of the Hong Kong Cultural Centre (see p82) on Thursday lunchtimes and some Saturdays. The Fringe Club (see p64) hosts free live music from local and visiting bands on certain weekends. Free exhibitions of local artists' and photographers' work are always on at the Hong Kong Arts Centre in Tsim Sha Tsui.

10 Bargain Basement Accommodation

For central and cheap, if admittedly sometimes nasty, accommodation, try the labyrinthine Chungking Mansions or its grubby little sister Mirador Mansions, both on Nathan Road in Tsim Sha Tsui. Also consider the YMCA and Youth Hostel Association (see also pp146, 151 & 152).

Directory

YMCA
2268 7888

Youth Hostel Association
2788 1638

Left **Cobbler** Centre **Landmark Centre** Right **Souvenir opera mask**

Shopping Tips

1 Opening Hours
Most shops open daily but not usually before about 10:30am and will not generally close before 6:30pm. Many, especially in the busy shopping districts, close later at 9pm or beyond.

2 Sales Tax
The government is considering a 3 per cent sales tax, but at present there is no sales tax apart from on cars, cosmetics, alcohol and tobacco.

3 When to Haggle
Small businesses, such as the many independent computer and electrical goods stores, are often worth trying to bargain with. Consider asking for a cash discount for items such as computers or antiques. Haggling is almost obligatory in the markets, particularly for gifts, antiques and souvenirs.

4 QTS Symbol
Where you see the QTS symbol (a large gold Q with black brushstroke), it indicates the shop has passed a Hong Kong Productivity Council Audit for fair trading, service levels, store environment and product knowledge.

5 Finding Larger Sizes
Some Westerners, women in particular, find shoes designed for the slighter Asian foot a tight fit. It's worth asking boutiques and shops if they have your size in their warehouse. Clothes are usually less of a problem. Hong Kong's Marks & Spencer outlets provide a wide range of clothing sizes.

6 Finding a Tailor
Dozens of tailors can hand-make suits in as little as 48 hours. The prices can be good, although a cheap deal sometimes means cheap cloth or corners cut. If in doubt use a better-known tailor. For men's suits try the famous Sam the Tailor or the Mandarin Hotel's bespoke A-Man Hing Cheong. For tailor-made *cheong sams*, try funky Shanghai Tang.

7 Shopping on a Budget
For dirt-cheap clothes, head to the markets at Lai Chi Kok and Sham Shui Po. The ubiquitous Giordano and Bossini chains offer decent, good value Gap-style wear. For deeply discounted clearance designer wear head to the shops on the 4th, 5th and 6th floors of the Pedder Building *(see p63)* in Central or Joyce's warehouse outlet on Ap Lei Chau *(see p76)*.

8 Break for the Border
Consider getting a visa for China *(see p136)* and cross over to the border town of Shenzhen *(see p126–9)* for cheap clothes and designer fakes. If you're prepared to haggle for each and every purchase and do a lot of shopping, the trip will pay for itself.

9 Fakes
Fake designer clothes and watches are cheap, common and easy to find in any of Hong Kong's markets and especially in Shenzhen. Quality can range from the good to the dreadful, so buyer beware.

10 Avoiding Rip-Offs
Take great care when buying complicated items such as cameras, computers and other electronics, particularly from the independent shops in Tsim Sha Tsui. Is there a warranty? If yes, can the item be serviced or repaired under it once you are back home? Are essential accessories included?

Directory

A-Man Hing Cheong
Mandarin Oriental, 5 Connaught Rd, Central, Hong Kong Island • 2522 3336

Sam the Tailor
94 Nathan Rd, Tsim Sha Tsui • 2367 9423

Shanghai Tang
12 Pedder St, Central, Hong Kong Island • 2525 7333

Left **Happy Valley** Right **Tsing Ma suspension bridge**

🔟 Tours

1 HKTB Bus-Based Tours

If time is short or legs tire, the five-hour Heritage Tour offers a whistlestop glimpse of ancient temples, ancestral clan halls and walled villages. The daily Land Between Tour takes in Hong Kong's highest mountain, rural markets and fishing villages. Book on the HKTB's reservations hotline.

2 Cultural Kaleidoscope

This innovative and free series of walks and lectures by a group of experts on local culture, traditional Chinese medicine and feng shui, offers some excellent insights into traditional Hong Kong and Chinese culture. A daily talk is held at a set location covering a different topic each day. Get details from the HKTB.

3 DIY Walking Tours

It may be a stone's throw from Central's skyscrapers, but the self-guided Western Walking Tour takes you into a different world past dried seafood shops, herbalists and temples. Pick up a brochure from HKTB offices. A more remote alternative is the Lung Yuek Tau Heritage Trail, a short but fascinating walk starting at Fung Ying Sin Koon Temple, which passes elegant ancestral halls, and tiny, still-inhabited walled villages.

4 Hong Kong Dolphinwatch

You're almost guaranteed to see Hong Kong's endangered pink dolphins off Lantau Island on this four-hour tour, and if you don't you can go again free. Learn from the knowledgeable guides about the lives of these creatures and the threats they face.

5 Museums and Galleries

See all of Hong Kong's museums and galleries the easy way via the bus that shuttles between the art, science, space and history museums in Tsim Sha Tsui and the smart, impressive new Heritage Museum at Sha Tin. A one-week bus pass with unlimited entry ticket to all museums is available from HKTB offices. The special bus runs on Wednesday, Friday and Sunday from 10am to 6pm.

6 Harbour Tours

Take in the skyline of Central from the harbour by day or night, or sail beneath the Tsing Ma suspension bridge. A range of harbour cruises is on offer. Visit HKTB offices for details.

7 Horseracing Tour

Feel the earth move and the hooves thunder as you cheer the finishers home in the ultimate Hong Kong night out. Splendid Tours runs the Come Horseracing Tour during race meetings (see pp12–13 & 101).

8 Local Rambles

Local historian Jason Wordie's weekly Detours column and the outward-bound Explore column in the *Sunday Morning Post Magazine* may provide inspiration and useful information on Hong Kong's hidden corners.

9 Junk Hire

If money is no object, hire a junk for the day and explore Hong Kong's secluded beaches and craggy islands. See the *Yellow Pages* for listings.

10 Helicopter Rides

For the most dramatic perspectives on Hong Kong, HKTB recommend Grayline Tours' 12-minute helicopter ride, followed by lunch on Jumbo Restaurant and a cruise from Jumbo to Stanley. Scenic Hong Kong Panorama offers a cruise to the Sai Kung Peninsula, helicopter ride and lunch.

Directory

HKTB Tours
Reservations hotline,
7am–9pm daily • 2508 1234

Hong Kong Dolphinwatch
2984 1414

Scenic Hong Kong Panorama
2723 1808

Left **YMCA** Centre **Waiter, Peninsula Hotel** Right **Lobby, Island Shangri-La**

TOP 10 Accommodation Tips

1 Making Reservations

Booking through the HKTB or a travel agent will almost always be cheaper than just turning up at a hotel. Many websites offer hotel reservation services *(see also p137)*. The Hong Kong Hotel Association runs information and reservations lines.

2 High Season

Rates climb during the busy conference months of October and April, and the best hotels (and many of the rest) will be booked solid. Avoid these months if you can, or book long in advance.

3 What's Included in the Price

Use of facilities such as gyms and pools are usually included in the room price. Breakfast is seldom included in the price except at top-of-the-range places. Note that a 3 per cent government tax and a 10 per cent service charge will be added to your bill at all but the lowest-priced guesthouses. Local calls are free from public phones in Hong Kong, but strangely not usually from your hotel room.

4 Good Cheap Accommodation

Don't be put off by the name, the YMCA *(see p151)* in Tsim Sha Tsui is well appointed and offers terrific views and value.

Or try the two-star Anne Black Guest House close to the Temple Street area in Kowloon. *(See also other entries pp151–2.)*

5 Late Arrivals

If you've just got off the plane and need a place, try the hotel information and reservations offices in arrivals halls A and B, open from 6am to 1pm or make for Chungking or Mirador Mansions on Nathan Road *(see p152)*.

6 Useful Websites

The websites listed in the directory are easy to use and book through, with plenty of substantial deals and discounts of up to 65 per cent.

7 Single Travellers

The Anne Black Guest House has plenty of clean, cheap single rooms. Less appealing (but half the price) guesthouses such as in the Chungking Mansions *(see p152)* are other good budget options for single travellers.

8 Families

Most of the better hotels offer babysitting services. The YMCA *(see p151)* has a few competitively priced family suites.

9 Long-Stay Deals

Many hotels and guesthouses will offer excellent discounts for stays of a month or

more. For long stays it may be worth renting a serviced apartment *(below)*. The Wesley in Wan Chai offers very competitive monthly packages. *(See also p153.)*

10 Apartotels

The TransAsia Group offers Central serviced apartments. If you want to get away from it all, some small, basic holiday apartments can be rented on leafy, low-rise Lamma Island close to the beaches, bars and restaurants.

Directory

Hong Kong Hotel Association
Information 2383 8380
• Reservations 2769 8822 • www.hkha.org

Anne Black Guest House
2713 9211

Websites
• www.asiahotels.com
• www.accomline.com
• www.asiatravel.com
• www.lastminute.com.hk
• www.rentaroomhk.com

TransAsia Group
2522 3082 • www.transasiagroup.com

YMCA
41 Salisbury Rd, Tsim Sha Tsui • 2268 7000

The Wesley
22 Hennessy Rd, Wan Chai • 2866 6688

eft **Bar Shangri-La** Right **The Mandarin Oriental**

₀10 Super Luxury Hotels

1 The Peninsula
Opened in 1928 and till one of Hong Kong's est-loved hotels, the Neo-Classical Peninsula over-poking Victoria Harbour s famous for restrained uxury and excellent, riendly service *(see 81)*. ◈ *Salisbury Rd, owloon • Map N4 • 2920 888 • www.peninsula.com $$$$$*

2 The Mandarin Oriental HK
 favourite among royalty, oliticians, stars and busi-ess folk, the Mandarin enefits from a supreme central location and a repu-ation for excellence and ld-fashioned opulence. eyond the imposing gold nd black marble lobby nd the frock-coated oncierges and bellhops, he Mandarin's elegant ooms have balconies verlooking the harbour nd, less happily, busy onnaught Road. ◈ *5 onnaught Rd, Central Map L5 • 2522 0111 • vww.mandarinoriental.com $$$$$*

3 Hotel Intercontinental Hong Kong
opular with the rich and amous, the splendid, hodern Intercontinental ormerly the Regent) is onsistently voted among sia's best hotels. The uge, beautifully appoint-d rooms offer fantastic arbour views. ◈ *18 Salisury Rd, Kowloon • Map V4 • 2721 1211 • www. terconti.com • $$$$$*

4 Island Shangri-La
The lovely airy lobby, huge chandeliers and stunning silk landscape adorning the atrium are a prelude to the largest hotel rooms in Hong Kong, with terrific Peak or harbour views. ◈ *Pacific Place, Central • Map M6 • 2877 3838 • www.shangri-la.com • $$$$$*

5 The Conrad
Guests are dwarfed by the giant flowers and insects on the high lobby murals in this impressive hotel. Rooms above the 40th floor are large and sumptuous, with excellent harbour or Peak views. ◈ *Pacific Place, Central • Map M6 • 2521 3838 • www.conrad. com.hk • $$$$$*

6 The Grand Hyatt
Next to the Convention Centre and the sole choice for unbridled luxury in Wanchai, the Grand Hyatt has looked after world-famous guests including former US President Clinton. Revamped rooms have a modern feel, including all high-tech mod-cons. ◈ *1 Harbour Rd, Wan Chai • Map N5 • 2588 1234 • www.hongkong.hyatt.com • $$$$$*

7 The Ritz-Carlton
Smaller and more intimate than many of its luxury heavyweight con-tenders, the plush, ele-gantly chintzy Ritz Carlton is celebrated for peerless, friendly service. ◈ *3 Connaught Rd, Central • Map L5 • 2877 6666 • www.ritzcarlton.com • $$$$$*

8 The Mandarin Oriental Macau
What this Mandarin lacks in its ferry terminal loca-tion it more than makes up for with service and facilities. It is, perhaps, the best hotel in Macau. Compared with Hong Kong's rates, this is luxury on the cheap. ◈ *956 1110 Avenida da Amizade, Macau • 567 888 • www.mandarin oriental.com • $$$*

9 Kowloon Shangri-La
Not quite up to the standards of its Hong Kong Island counterpart, perhaps, but the Kowloon Shangri-La offers luxury at a significant discount to its sister. The Horizon Club tariff includes butler service and club lounge. ◈ *64 Mody Rd, Kowloon • Map P3 • 2721 2111 • www.shangri-la.com • $$$$$*

10 The Langham
Restrained opulence reigns throughout. There's a good gym, pool and sauna and top-quality restaurants, including the impressive Cantonese T'ang Court, decked out like a Mongolian tent. ◈ *8 Peking Road, Tsim Sha Tsui, Kowloon • Map M3 • 2375 1133 • www.langham hotels.com • $$$$*

Note: *Unless otherwise stated, all hotels accept credit cards, have en-suite bathrooms and air conditioning*

Left **Holiday Inn Golden Mile** Centre **The Sheraton** Right **Regal Airport Hotel**

🔟 Luxury Hotels

1 The Lisboa

Behind its audacious (some might say tasteless) exterior are more than 900 large rooms with beautifully embroidered bedspreads and great views. Dripping with marble and gilt, this temple to excess contains several casinos and top-notch fine dining. 🕲 *2-4 Avenida de Lisboa, Macau • 853 577666 • www. hotelisboa.com • \$\$\$*

2 Holiday Inn Golden Mile

Located in the heart of Kowloon's shopping Golden Mile, the Holiday Inn has a wide range of eating and drinking options, many at reasonable prices. Rooms are comfortable, but won't win any prizes. Facilities include pool, gym and babysitting service. 🕲 *50 Nathan Rd, Tsim Sha Tsui • Map N2 • 2369 3111 • www.goldenmile-hk.holiday-inn.com • \$\$\$\$*

3 China Hotel Guangzhou

Possibly outdone by the equally huge Garden Hotel, China Hotel is still up in the top three hotels in Guangzhou and hogs the prime spot next to the city's Trade Fair ground. There's a large, well-equipped gym, health centre, outdoor pool and a vast range of decent restaurants and cafés. 🕲 *Liu Hua Lu, Guangzhou • (8620) 8666 6888 • \$\$\$*

4 Royal Garden Hotel

The 20-year-old Royal Garden is ageing beautifully, partly due to a recent facelift. Elegant rooms with cable TV sit round the bright atrium lobby. The rooftop gym, pool and tennis court impress, as does the world-class Italian restaurant. 🕲 *69 Mody Rd, Tsim Sha Tsui • Map P3 • 2721 5215 • www.theroyalgarden hotel.com.hk • \$\$\$\$*

5 Garden Hotel Guangzhou

The cavernous lobby gives some sense of the size of this imposing 1,000-plus room hotel, boasting its own up-market shopping mall and good eating and drinking options. 🕲 *368 Huangshi Dong Lu, Guangzhou • (8620) 8333 8989 • www.gardenhotel-guangzhou.com • \$\$\$*

6 The Park Lane

Room sizes are generous, most with views. Surf the net via your TV with wireless keyboard. Revamped deluxe rooms are very funky, especially the glass-walled bathrooms with glass sinks. 🕲 *310 Gloucester Rd, Causeway Bay • Map Q5 • 2293 8888 • www.parklane. com.hk • \$\$\$\$*

7 The Excelsior

The smart, modern and friendly Excelsior offers pretty much every in-room and hotel facility imaginable, as you'd expect from the Mandarin Oriental's sister. 🕲 *281 Gloucester Rd, Causeway Bay • Map Q5 • 2894 8888 • www.excelsiorhongkong. com • \$\$\$\$*

8 The Sheraton

Rooms are comfortable but hardly special. However, the hotel's central waterfront position, and full range of facilities including gym, pool, spa and 24-hour movie channels, put it in the luxury category. 🕲 *20 Nathan Rd, Kowloon • Map N4 • 2369 1111 • www.sheraton.com/ hongkong • \$\$\$\$\$*

9 Shangri-La Hotel Shenzhen

Close to the main shopping areas and railway station, the Shangri-la makes a great escape from Shenzhen's seething retail madness. The rooftop pool (with gym, sauna and steam room nearby) makes a good place to relax. 🕲 *Shenzhen • Map D1 • (86 755) 233 0888 • www.shangri-la.com • \$\$\$*

🔟 Harbour Plaza

The Hung Hom location is the main problem with this otherwise terrific hotel. Rooms have large beds and plush bathrooms, some with fine harbour views. There's a splendid glass-sided rooftop pool. 🕲 *Hung Hom • Map Q3 • 2621 3188 • www.harbour-plaza.com • \$\$\$*

Note: *Unless otherwise stated, all hotels accept credit cards, have en-suite bathrooms and air conditioning*

Left **Kowloon Hotel** Right **The Kimberley Hotel**

Price Categories		
For a standard, double room per night (with breakfast if included), taxes and extra charges.	**$** under HK$500
	$$ HK$500–$1,000
	$$$ HK$1,000–$2,000
	$$$$ HK$2,000–$2,500
	$$$$$ over HK$2,500

🔟 Mid-Range Hotels in Hong Kong

1 The Renaissance Harbour View
The location above the Convention and Exhibition Centre on the waterfront insures its popularity as a business hotel. Other visitors will like its landscaped grounds, leisure facilities and reasonable rates. ◈ 1 Harbour Rd, Wanchai • Map N5 • 2802 888 • www.renaissancehotels.com • $$$

2 Kowloon Hotel
Less opulent than its sister hotel, the Peninsula across the way, the Kowloon is more suited to people seeking good location and connectivity. Its high-tech rooms boast computers with Internet access. Rooms are smallish though, and the supposedly digital/techlook is starting to look unintentionally retro 80s. ◈ 19–21 Nathan Road, Tsim Sha Tsui, Kowloon • Map N4 • 2929 2888 • www.peninsula.com • $$$

3 Empire Hotel Kowloon
Opened in late 2001, this very smart hotel with modern gym and lovely atrium pool is a complete contrast to its threadbare sister in Wanchai. Rooms are equipped with the latest Internet and audiovisual gadgetry. Well located for Tsim Sha Tsui shopping and dining. ◈ 62 Kimberley Road, Tsim Sha Tsui • Map N3 • 2685 3000 • www.asiastandard.com • $$$

4 The Kimberley Hotel
The impressive, marbled lobby contains a business centre, pleasant bar and café lounge area around a soothing waterfall and lily pond. Rooms are well appointed, with marble bathrooms. Facilities include a golf driving range and spa. ◈ 28 Kimberley Rd, Tsim Sha Tsui • Map N3 • 2723 3888 • www.Kimberley.com.hk • $$$

5 Regal Airport Hotel
Hong Kong's largest hotel links directly to the airport terminal and features large rooms with avant-garde interior designs. Ten restaurants and bars provide a choice of cuisine. ◈ 9 Cheong Tat Rd, Chek Lap Kok • Map B5 • 2286 8888 • www.regalhotel.com • $$$

6 Hotel Miramar
A high-quality hotel in every respect. Despite the Nathan Road location, noise won't be a problem as the rooms are well sound-proofed. The gym and pool are modern and impressive and there's a good selection of restaurants. ◈ 118-130 Nathan Rd, Tsim Sha Tsui • Map N3 • 2368 1111 • www.miramarhk.com • $$$

7 Imperial Hotel
Unbeatable for location in TST, the Imperial offers average-priced rooms, with discounts of up to 30 per cent when occupancy is low. Rooms are adequate but there are no other facilities except a small business centre. ◈ 30–34 Nathan Rd, Tsim ShaTsui • Map N4 • 2366 2201 • www.imperial hotel.com.hk • $$$

8 The Eaton Hotel
Easily the best option in the Yau Ma Tei/Jordan area. Rooms are smart, with broadband access, fax machine, bath and separate shower. The lobby offers a flood of natural light, outdoor seating and a lovely oasis of greenery. ◈ 380 Nathan Rd • Map N1 • 2782 1818 • www.eaton-hotel.com • $$$

9 New World Renaissance
With adequate rooms and basic facilities, this competitively priced hotel is worth considering, although its interiors are in need of a facelift. Special deals and 50 per cent discounts are available. ◈ 22 Salisbury Rd, Tsim Sha Tsui • Map N4 • 2369 4111 • www.renaissancehotels. com • $$$

🔟 Bishop Lei International House
It's quiet and close to the park. Rooms are small for the money – but you pay for proximity to the Escalator. Long stay packages are available. ◈ 4 Robinson Rd, Mid-Levels • Map K6 • 2868 0828 • www.bishop leihtl.com.hk • $$$

Left **Holiday Inn Macau** Centre **The Metropole** Right **New Century Hotel**

TOP 10 Mid-Range Hotels, Macau & Chin

1 Holiday Inn

Close by Lisboa's many casinos and convenient for the centre of Macau. Rooms (with cable) are blandly furnished but there's a good range of facilities, including gym, pool, sauna and a decent restaurant for Cantonese and Szechuan food. ✆ 82–86 Rua de Pequin, Macau • (853) 783 333 • www.holiday-inn.com • $$$

2 The Metropole

The sense that you've travelled back to the 1970s can be fun, but apart from that, this ageing hotel, aimed more at Chinese mainlanders than foreigners, is nothing special. Happily, prices are low and it's next to some of Macau's best shopping and sightseeing areas. ✆ 70 Avenida do Dr Rodrigo Rodrigues, Macau • (853) 780822 • $$

3 Hotel Royal Macau

The Hotel Royal is one of Macau's oldest hotels and shows it. That said, it is clean and well run, although the rooms offer little more than the basics. It has an indoor pool, gym (with some ageing equipment) and sauna. It's also close to the heart of town and within sight of the pretty Guia Lighthouse. ✆ 2-4 Estrada da Vitoria, Macau • Map ref • (853) 552 222 • www.hotelroyal.com.mo • $$

4 New Century Hotel

Heavy on the marble and chintz, this is unmistakably a gambling hotel. For non-gamblers it's put in the shade somewhat by the lovely Hyatt opposite, but does offer comprehensive guest facilities. Rooms are big and have satellite TV. ✆ 889 Av. Padre Tomas Periera, Taipa, Macau • (853) 831111 • $$$

5 Guangdong Victory Hotel

Formerly the Victoria Hotel, this concern occupies two sites on Shamian Island – the main, new Neo-Classical block and the original colonial building. Facilities include business centre, swimming pool and sauna. ✆ 53 Shamian St North, Guangzhou • (8620) 8186 2622 • www.gd-victory-hotel.com • $$

6 Guangdong Hotel, Shenzhen

A reasonably good value option with comfortable, if basic, rooms. Fairly thin on facilities, but with a modest restaurant and smart Japanese-style business centre. ✆ 3033 Shannandong Rd, Shenzhen (86 755) 2228339 • $$

7 Century Plaza Hotel

A decent hotel in the heart of Shenzhen with spacious rooms, cable TV, pool, sauna, gym and high-rise karaoke club. ✆ Kin Chit Rd Shenzhen • (86755) 232 0888 • www.szcentury plaza.com • $$$

8 Landmark Hotel, Shenzhen

This recently renovated hotel offers luxury and extensive facilities, including health club, driving range, gym and Internet room. ✆ 3018 Nanhu Rd, Shenzhen • (86 755) 217 2288 • $$$

9 The Panglin Hotel

Smart, modern and large, the Panglin is one of Shenzhen's superior hotels, about two miles (4 km) from the railway station. Room sizes are decent and all come with cable TV. Extensive services include station shuttle bus, baby-sitting and 24-hour room service. The revolving Skylounge at the top is Shenzhen's highest restaurant. ✆ 2002 Jiabin Road, Lowu, Shenzhen • (86 755) 518 5888 • www. panglin-hotel.com • $$$

10 Forum Hotel

This decent and good-value hotel is reasonably well located and even boasts its own art gallery. Standards are high (it's run by the Inter Continental Group), there are four restaurants, a gym, pool and sauna. ✆ 1085 Heping Road • (86 755) 558 6333 • www.intercontinenti • $$$

For maps of Macau, Shenzhen and Guangzhou See pp118, 126 & 130

Nathan Road

Price Categories

For a standard, double room per night (with breakfast if included), taxes and extra charges.

$	under HK$500
$$	HK$500–$1,000
$$$	HK$1,000–$2,000
$$$$	HK$2,000–$2,500
$$$$$	over HK$2,500

🔟 Value-for-Money Hotels

1 The Salisbury YMCA

Don't be put off by the initials. For value, views and location, the always-popular YMCA, next door to the posh Peninsula, can't be beaten. The well-furnished rooms are spacious, equipped with fax/laptop ports, satellite and cable TV. A large swimming pool, sauna, gym and indoor climbing wall round off the facilities. Family suites are terrific. A few excellent up-market dorm beds, too. ◉ 41 Salisbury Rd, Tsim Sha Tsui • Map M4 • 2268 7000 www.ymcahk.org.hk • $$

2 BP International House

The boxy rooms with ugly 80s wallpaper have smallish beds, but the place is clean, efficient and can be cheap, and has lovely views over Kowloon Park. ◉ 8 Austin Rd, Tsim Sha Tsui • Map M2 • 2376 1111 • www.bpih. com.hk • $$

3 The Wharney

Right in the increasingly smart centre of Wanchai, the Wharney offers decent surroundings, a revamped gym and pool, sauna, business centre and a couple of restaurants. Rooms are well appointed but on the small side. ◉ 57-73 Lockhart Road, Wanchai • Map N6 • 2861 1000 • www.wharney.gdhotels.net • $$$

4 The Wesley

Definitely the poor relation of the Grand Hotel Group's hotels, the Wesley's saving grace is its central location and low rates. That said, the fittings are tired and the rooms small. There's no pool or gym and only a modest café. ◉ 22 Hennessey Rd, Wanchai • Map N6 • 2866 6688 • $$

5 Garden View International House

Given the location, the prices aren't bad, and even better for long stays (two weeks plus). The décor is depressing 80s and the rooms smallish. Discounts of 30 to 50 per cent are often available in low season. ◉ 1 Macdonnell Rd • Map K6 • 2877 3737 • $$$

6 Shamrock

The rather severe lobby opens directly onto Nathan Road, and the dishevelled lifts lead up to some big rooms with satellite TV, a/c and telephone. ◉ 23 Nathan Rd • Map N4 • 2735 2271 • $$

7 Harbour View International House

This modest Chinese YMCA-run hotel charges a hefty premium for the location given the basic rooms, although low-season discounts are available. Bathtubs are only big enough for very supple adults. ◉ 4 Harbour Rd, Wanchai • Map N5 • 2802 0111 • $$$

8 2 Macdonnell Road

With pleasant rooms, a good Central location and excellent views across the Zoological and Botanical Gardens to the city and harbour, Macdonell Road offers good value for its position. Rooms have all the basics plus kitchenette. Long-stay packages are available (see p153). ◉ 2 Macdonnell Rd, Central • Map K6 • 2132 2132 $$$

9 The Empire Hotel

Marooned between the area's two main roads, the Empire is right in the heart of Wanchai so you're paying for location rather than luxury as the cheap, nasty fittings will constantly remind you. Still, prices are competitive, the service isn't bad and there's a small but adequate rooftop pool plus gym and broadband Internet access. ◉ 33 Hennessey Rd, Wan Chai • Map N6 • 2866 9111 • $$

10 Rosedale on the Park

One of Hong Kong's newest hotels, this self-styled "cyber boutique hotel" offers reasonable value. The look is sleek and modern, and the technology up to the minute. Small but well laid out rooms include broadband connection. ◉ 8 Shelter St, Causeway Bay • Map Q6 • 2127 8888 • www. rosedale.com.hk • $$$

Streetsmart

Left **Plover Cove** Right **The notorious Chungking House**

🔟 Cheap Sleeps

1 Anne Black Guest House

If location isn't important then consider the YWCA-run Anne Black Guest House stuck out in Mongkok. The rooms (either with private or communal bathrooms) are basic but clean with air-conditioning, TV, and telephone. 🕲 *5 Man Fuk Rd, Kowloon • Map E4 • 2713 9211 • www.ywca. org.hk • $$*

2 Booth Lodge

Air-conditioned rooms with shower, fridge, phone, bath and TV are merely adequate but the location and prices are great at this Salvation Army-run hotel. 🕲 *11 Wing Sing Lane, Yau Ma Tei, Kowloon • Map N1 • 2771 9266 • www.boothlodge. salvation.org.hk • $$*

3 Caritas Bianchi Lodge

Like Booth Lodge next door, there's only a chapel and restaurant-cum-café to amuse yourself here. Still, the rates are lower, and the rooms are large by any standards. 🕲 *4 Cliff Road, Yau Ma Tei, Kowloon • Map N1 • 2388 1111 • $$*

4 New King's Hotel

Well situated but in something of a chaotic, scrappy and noisy area. Rooms are neat but small, and the views unlovely. 🕲 *473 Nathan Rd, Yau Ma Tei, Kowloon • Map N1 • 2780 1281 • $$*

5 Holy Carpenter Guest House

A pleasant alternative to the dingier guesthouse offerings in Chungking and Mirador, but stuck out in boring old Hung Hom. Facilities in double and triple rooms are basic but include TV, phone, bathroom, shower and air-conditioning. 🕲 *1 Dyer Ave, Hung Hom, Kowloon • Map R2 • 2362 0301 • $$*

6 Bradbury Hall Hostel

As you might expect from such a remote hostel, basic, barrack-like dorms are the order of the day. Those with tents may want to walk on and pitch camp at Tai Long Wan's lovely beaches nearby. 🕲 *Chek Keng, Sai Kung, New Territories • Map F3 • 2328 2458 • $*

7 Bradbury Lodge Youth Hostel

This very pleasant hostel by the reservoir makes for a good base or stop-off for walkers wanting to explore the beautiful country around Plover Cove. Air-conditioned singles, doubles or dorms are available. 🕲 *Tai Mei Tuk, New Territories • Map F2 • 2662 5123 • $*

8 Pak Sha O Hostel

Lying in the heart of the country park, this is a functional hikers' overnight stop with dorm beds. The views are great and it's also possible to camp. 🕲 *Pak Sah O, Hoi Ha Rd, New Territories • Map F2 • 2328 2327 • $*

9 Sze Lok Yuen Hostel

A very basic hikers' crash-pad, Sze Lok Yuen perches close to the summit of Tai Mo Shan, Hong Kong's tallest peak. The views are spectacular but its dorm rooms are pretty basic with no fans or air-conditioning. The altitude cools things down though in all but the hottest months. Camping is permitted. 🕲 *Tai Mo Shan, Tseun Wan, New Territories • Map D3 • 2488 8188 • $*

10 Chungking House, Chungking Mansions

Staying at the mansions is a badge of honour to some budget travellers, an unpleasant necessity to others *(see p82)*. The dingy hallways and semi-squalor contain dozens of guesthouses offering cheap, boxy and usually stuffy accommodation in an excellent location. Oppressive and fascinating at the same time, Chungking Mansions is a warren of small-scale commerce and Hong Kong's cultural melting pot. Chungking House is probably the best option, with larger, more comfortable rooms than elsewhere in Chungking Mansions. 🕲 *Block 4A/5F, 40 Nathan Rd, Tsim Sha Tsui • Map N4 • 2366 5362 • $$*

Note: Unless otherwise stated, all hotels accept credit cards, have en-suite bathrooms and air conditioning

Price Categories

For a standard, double room per night (with breakfast if included), taxes and extra charges.

$	under HK$500
$$	HK$500–$1,000
$$$	HK$1,000–$2,000
$$$$	HK$2,000–$2,500
$$$$$	over HK$2,500

The Repulse Bay

≋10 Long-Stay Hotels

1 22 Peel St
Centrally located above a bustling produce market, this modern block offers cosy studios and spacious-looking apartments with smart furnishings, big beds, daily maid service and, for HK$250 extra, monthly unlimited broadband internet access. ✆ 22 Peel St, Central • Map K5 • 2522 3082 • HK$23,200–$50,000 per month

2 The Wesley
The fittings are tired and the rooms small, but The Wesley's saving grace is its very competitive long-stay packages in a central location. Deals include free local calls, maid service, kitchenette, and use of swimming pool and gym at the sister hotel in Quarry Bay. ✆ 22 Hennessey Rd, Wanchai • Map N6 • 2866 6688 • HK$7800–HK$25,000 per month

3 2 Macdonnell Road
Offering significantly smarter and only slightly pricier long-stay accommodation than next door's Garden View. The location is excellent; the views to the city and harbour good. Maid service, free local calls, use of gym, satellite and cable TV, kitchenette and Central shuttle bus are all included in the price. ✆ 2 Macdonnell Rd, Central • Map K6 • 2132 2132 • HK$16,500–HK$25,000 per month

4 The Atrium
Beautifully furnished, upmarket, executive apartments with five-star hotel-style service including health club, outdoor heated pool, 24-hour room service. Well located above Pacific Place with amazing views over the city. ✆ Pacific Place, 88 Queensway • Map M6 • 2844 8361 • HK$43,000–HK$105,000 per month

5 The Repulse Bay
For executives or small families, these upmarket two-bedroom duplex apartments are a 20-minute ride from Central in serene Repulse Bay. The big hole in one of the tower blocks promotes good feng shui apparently. ✆ Repulse Bay • Map E5 • 2812 7405 • www.the repulsebay.com • HK$65,000–HK$80,000 per month

6 The Bay Bridge
Given the Tsuen Wan location, these studio and suite apartments are not for those who must be at the centre of things. The apartments are smart, with shower and kitchenette. ✆ 123 Castle Peak Rd, Yau Kom Tau, Tsuen Wan, Kowloon • Map D3 • 2945 1111 • HK$6,800–HK$12,500 per month

7 The Staunton
Roll out of bed in these well decked out but small studio and one- or two-bed apartments and you're beside the Escalator, bars and restaurants. Homely, with smart fittings and Chinese decorative touches. ✆ Staunton Street, Central • Map K5 • 2522 3082 • HK$18,000–HK$25,000 per month

8 Garden View International House
Very competitive long-stay deals start at two weeks' duration. But décor is tired 80s, and the rooms smallish. Long stayers benefit from maid service, free local calls and Central shuttle bus. ✆ 1 Macdonnell Rd • Map K6 • 2877 3737 • HK$1,000 • $$$

9 The Rosedale on the Park
The shiny new Rosedale has small but well laid-out rooms with broadband connection and kitchenette. There's also a small gym. Causeway Bay's department stores and Victoria Park's many facilities are nearby. ✆ 8 Shelter St, Causeway Bay • Map Q6 • 2127 8639 • HK$14,500 per month

10 La Salle Court
The studio and one- and two-bedroom apartments are furnished with TV, fridge, cooker and oven. There's no gym or pool. but the park nearby has a public pool. ✆ 30 La Salle Rd, Kowloon Tong • Map E4 • 2338 38999 • HK$7000–HK$28,000 per month

Left The Warwick **Right** Restaurant, Harbour Plaza

Price Categories

For a standard, double room per night (with breakfast if included), taxes and extra charges.	**$** under HK$500
	$$ HK$500–$1,000
	$$$ HK$1,000–$2,000
	$$$$ HK$2,000–$2,500
	$$$$$ over HK$2,500

TOP 10 Great Escapes

1 Hong Kong Gold Coast Hotel

This ten-acre resort offers sea views from its well-equipped rooms. The accommodation complex is unlovely from outside, and you won't be swimming in crystal waters, but recreation facilities include pool, pitch-and-putt golf course, tennis courts and running track. ⊗ *No.1 Castle Peak Rd, Kowloon • Map B3 • 2452 8888 HK$1,250 • $$$*

2 The Warwick

A cheap alternative to city living, magical Cheung Chau's only major hotel offers fine sea views next to good beaches with windsurf and kayak hire. Great coastal walks are around the headland. Furnishings are nothing special, and the exterior is 60s municipal. ⊗ *East Bay, Cheung Chau • Map C6 • 2981 0081 • $$*

3 Harbour Plaza Resort City

Out in the New Territories, this extensive resort complex offers a chance to escape city living with a vast array of sports and recreation facilities, including cinemas, shops, gyms, sports tracks and courts, Chinese and International restaurants, and nearby historical and beauty spots. All rooms include the basics with lounge and kitchenette. ⊗ *18 Yin Ngam Rd, Tin Shui Wai, New Territories • Map C2 • 2180 6688 • $$*

4 Jockey Club Mount Davis Youth Hostel

An excellent budget option for the adventurous, this lovely, clean and friendly hostel sits atop Mount Butler at the western edge of Hong Kong Island. Take a taxi there. ⊗ *Mount Davis Path, Kennedy Town • Map D5 • 2817 5715 • $*

5 Concerto Inn

Hardly a resort hotel but worth a night's escape to leafy, low-rise Lamma Island. Modest but neat air-conditioned rooms with TV and minibar. Lamma's famous Han Lok Yuen pigeon restaurant is nearby (see p117). ⊗ *Hung Shing Ye, Lamma Island • Map D6 • 2982 1668 • $$*

6 White Swan Hotel

Overlooking the Pearl River on sleepy Shamian Island, this large but lovely hotel is the place to find peace in Guangzhou. Rooms are smart; the beds large. ⊗ *1 Southern St, Shamian Island, Guangzhou • (86 20) 8188 6968 • $$$*

7 Pousada de Sao Taigo

Converted from an old Portuguese fort hewn from the rock in the 17th century, this tiny hotel looking across the bay to mainland China is a picturesque delight. Rooms are heavily but beautifully decorated in Portuguese style. ⊗ *Avenida de Republica, Fortaleza de Sao Tiago de Barra, Macau • 378 111 • $$$*

8 Westin Macau

A lovely getaway. All rooms come with own terrace and sea views. There's a small sandy beach and an 18-hole golf course, which hosts the Macau Open. Or practise your swing with a bucket of balls on the ocean driving range. Yes, these ones float. ⊗ *1918 Estrada de Hac Sa, Ilha de Coloane, Macau • 871 111 • $$$*

9 Hyatt Regency Macau

A great, family-friendly resort-style hotel. Lovely Portuguese-style rooms, all with sea views and featuring minimalist décor with Oriental touches. Fantastic pastries and desserts are baked on the premises. ⊗ *2 Estrada Almirante, Taipa Island, Macau • 83 1234 •www.hyatt.com • $$$*

10 Pousada de Coloane

Tiny, remote, hotel at the far end of Coloane overlooking a small, pretty beach. It boasts a nice deck area, swimming pool, and attractive Portuguese-style restaurant and bar. Room fittings show their age, but they are well equipped. ⊗ *Chok Van Beach, Coloane Island, Macau • 882143 • $$*

Note: *Unless otherwise stated, all hotels accept credit cards, have en-suite bathrooms and air conditioning*

General Index

Acknowledgements

The Authors
Jason Gagliardi is a freelance travel writer who divides his time between Hong Kong and Bangkok; Liam Fitzpatrick works for the Hong Kong Tourist Board and lives in London; Andrew Stone is a freelance travel writer based in Hong Kong.

Produced by Blue Island Publishing, Highbury, London
Editorial Director Rosalyn Thiro
Art Director Stephen Bere
Picture Research Ellen Root
Research Assistance Amaia Allende
Proofread and Index Michael Ellis
Fact Checker Emily White

Main Photographers
Nigel Hicks, Chris Stowers

Additional Photography
Dave King, Steven Lam, David McIntyre, David Murray, Jules Selmes, Paul Williams

Artwork Lee Redmond

Cartography James Macdonald, Mapping Ideas Ltd

AT DORLING KINDERSLEY:
Senior Publishing Manager Louise Lang
Publishing Manager Kate Poole
Senior Art Editor Marisa Renzullo
Director of Publishing Gillian Allan
Publisher Douglas Amrine
Cartography Co-ordinator Casper Morris
DTP Jason Little, Conrad van Dyk
Production Sarah Dodd

Picture Credits
The publishers would like to thank all the museums, hotels, restaurants, bars, clubs, casinos, shops, galleries and other sights for their assistance and kind permission to photograph at their establishments.

Placement Key: t=top; tl=top left; tr=top right; tc=top centre; trc=top right centre; c=centre; ca=centre above; cra=centre right above; cb=centre below; cr=centre right; b=bottom; bra=bottom right above; bl=bottom left; br=bottom right; l=left
CORBIS: Bettmann 30tc/bl; Horace Bristol 30br; Adam Woolfitt 119t;

Courtesy of THE HARBOUR PLAZA: 154tc; NIGEL HICKS: 8–9, 44tc/br, 47tl, 72tc, 78–9, 102tr, 110–1;
Courtesy of the HONG KONG HERITAGE MUSEUM: 7ca, 20tr, 21ca;
Courtesy of the HONG KONG TOURISM BOARD: 8l, 14tl/b, 28c, 30tl, 32tl/tc/c/b, 33tl/tc/tr/bl, 34c, 35t, 36tl/tc/tr/c/b, 37tl/tr/cra/cr/bra/br, 40tc/tr, 44tl/tr/c/bl, 46tr, 50tc, 72tl, 80tl/c, 83tl, 103tr/cr, 116tr, 137tl, 138t, 139tl/tc/tr, 141tl/tc/tr, 142tl, 143tr, 144tl, 145tl/tr, 146tl/tc, 148tr;

Courtesy of the ISLAND SHANGRI-LA: 147tl;

Courtesy of the KIMBERLEY HOTEL: 149tc; Courtesy of the KOWLOON HOTEL: 149tl;

Courtesy of the MANDARIN ORIENTAL HOTEL: 147tc; Courtesy of THE MACAU GOVERNMENT TOURIST OFFICE:137tc, 150tl/tc/tr;

NATIONAL MARITIME MUSEUM, London: 30c;

PANOS PICTURES: Chris Stowers 3tr, 8b, 14tr, 18–19, 19t, 30tr, 31t, 34tr, 38br, 63tl, 66c/tr, 75tr, 88tl, 152tr; Courtesy of the PENINSULA HOTEL: 146tr;

Courtesy of the SHERATON HONG KONG: 148tc;

Courtesy of the WARWICK HOTEL: 154tl.

All other images are © Dorling Kindersley. For further information see *www.dkimages.com*.

Cartography Credits
Cartography derived from Bartholomew Digital Database, www.bartholomewmaps.com.

Acknowledgements